Cambridge Elements ≡

Elements in Public Engagement with Science
edited by
Angela Potochnik
University of Cincinnati
Melissa Jacquart
University of Cincinnati

BUILDING CAPACITY FOR PUBLIC ENGAGEMENT ON SOLAR GEOENGINEERING

Sikina Jinnah
University of California, Santa Cruz

Zachary Dove
University of California, Santa Cruz

Shuchi Talati
The Alliance for Just Deliberation on Solar Geoengineering

Erika Check Hayden
University of California, Santa Cruz

Alice Siu
Stanford University

Mahmud Farooque
Arizona State University

CAMBRIDGE
UNIVERSITY PRESS

Shaftesbury Road, Cambridge CB2 8EA, United Kingdom

One Liberty Plaza, 20th Floor, New York, NY 10006, USA

477 Williamstown Road, Port Melbourne, VIC 3207, Australia

314–321, 3rd Floor, Plot 3, Splendor Forum, Jasola District Centre,
New Delhi – 110025, India

Cambridge University Press is part of Cambridge University Press & Assessment,
a department of the University of Cambridge.

We share the University's mission to contribute to society through the pursuit of
education, learning and research at the highest international levels of excellence.

www.cambridge.org
Information on this title: www.cambridge.org/9781009632829

DOI: 10.1017/9781009632836

© Sikina Jinnah, Zachary Dove, Shuchi Talati, Erika Check Hayden, Alice Siu, and
Mahmud Farooque 2026

This publication is in copyright. Subject to statutory exception and to the provisions
of relevant collective licensing agreements, with the exception of the Creative
Commons version the link for which is provided below, no reproduction of any part
may take place without the written permission of Cambridge University Press &
Assessment.

An online version of this work is published at doi.org/10.1017/9781009632836 under
a Creative Commons Open Access license CC-BY-NC 4.0 which permits re-use,
distribution and reproduction in any medium for non-commercial purposes providing
appropriate credit to the original work is given and any changes made are indicated.
To view a copy of this license visit https://creativecommons.org/licenses/by-nc/4.0

When citing this work, please include a reference to the DOI 10.1017/9781009632836

First published 2026

A catalogue record for this publication is available from the British Library

*A Cataloging-in-Publication data record for this Element is available from the
Library of Congress*

ISBN 978-1-009-63282-9 Hardback
ISBN 978-1-009-63278-2 Paperback
ISSN 2753-7137 (online)
ISSN 2753-7129 (print)

Additional resources for this publication at www.cambridge.org/jinnah-et-al

Cambridge University Press & Assessment has no responsibility for the persistence
or accuracy of URLs for external or third-party internet websites referred to in this
publication and does not guarantee that any content on such websites is, or will remain,
accurate or appropriate.

For EU product safety concerns, contact us at Calle de José Abascal, 56, 1°, 28003
Madrid, Spain, or email eugpsr@cambridge.org

Building Capacity for Public Engagement on Solar Geoengineering

Elements in Public Engagement with Science

DOI: 10.1017/9781009632836
First published online: April 2026

Sikina Jinnah
University of California, Santa Cruz

Zachary Dove
University of California, Santa Cruz

Shuchi Talati
The Alliance for Just Deliberation on Solar Geoengineering

Erika Check Hayden
University of California, Santa Cruz

Alice Siu
Stanford University

Mahmud Farooque
Arizona State University

Author for correspondence: Sikina Jinnah, sjinnah@ucsc.edu

Abstract: Solar geoengineering (SG) is a set of highly controversial emerging technologies proposed to address climate change by reflecting sunlight away from the planet to reduce temperatures. SG may reduce climate risks; however, it also presents novel risks, uncertainties, and challenges, necessitating broad and inclusive public engagement. This Element presents a briefing book and methods toolkit to build capacity for public engagement on SG. Part I of the Element explains the need to build capacity to enable public engagement on solar geoengineering and presents three methods for doing so: capacity building workshops, participatory Technology Assessment, and Deliberative Polling. Part II presents a briefing book that provides accessible, balanced, and evidence-based information on critical topics, including climate science, climate policy, SG science, SG governance and policy, and SG ethics and justice. This title is also available as open access on Cambridge Core.

Keywords: solar geoengineering, capacity building, public engagement, science communication, climate justice

ISBNs: 9781009632829 (HB), 9781009632782 (PB), 9781009632836 (OC)
ISSNs: 2753-7137 (online), 2753-7129 (print)

Contents

With gratitude, inspiration, and love we dedicate this Element to the late Dr. Pablo Suarez who had an unparalleled gift for connection and engagement.

Part I Introduction and Methods

1 Introduction

If we had a reliable way to label our toys good and bad, it would be easy to regulate technology wisely. But we can rarely see far enough ahead to know which road leads to damnation. Whoever concerns [them]self with big technology, either to push it forward or to stop it, is gambling in human lives.

–Freeman Dyson, Disturbing the Universe (1979)

1.1 Setting the Stage

Solar geoengineering (SG) is a highly controversial emerging technology that might be used to address climate change by reflecting sunlight away from the planet to reduce global temperatures. There are several technologies that might achieve this goal, including stratospheric aerosol injection, which proposes to use high-altitude aircraft to deposit reflective aerosols in the stratosphere; and marine cloud brightening, which would increase the reflectivity of clouds over the ocean, among others (Figure 1). In theory, SG could mimic what happens when a large-scale volcanic eruption deposits sulfur in the atmosphere. For example, in the fifteen months following the 2001 eruption of Mount Pinatubo in the Philippines, scientists observed a 1 degree Fahrenheit (0.6 degree C) reduction in global average surface temperatures (NASA, 2001).[1] The hypothesis of SG as a climate response is premised on this dynamic. If government failure to address climate change continues, and climate change impacts continue to accelerate, could humans mimic what volcanoes do to cool the planet? It's a scary proposition. But so is doing nothing.

SG is currently only an idea. Now is the time to shape what SG could be if ever fully developed. In this Element we offer guidance on how people can engage SG with an eye toward making research and decision-making more responsive to the values, concerns, hopes, and knowledge of broad groups of publics. We explain the controversies, outline why public engagement is so important, share why capacity building is needed to enable public engagement,

---

[1] This Element cites several US government websites throughout. Historical versions of government websites that are altered or removed can be found using the GovWayback tool available at: https://govwayback.com/.

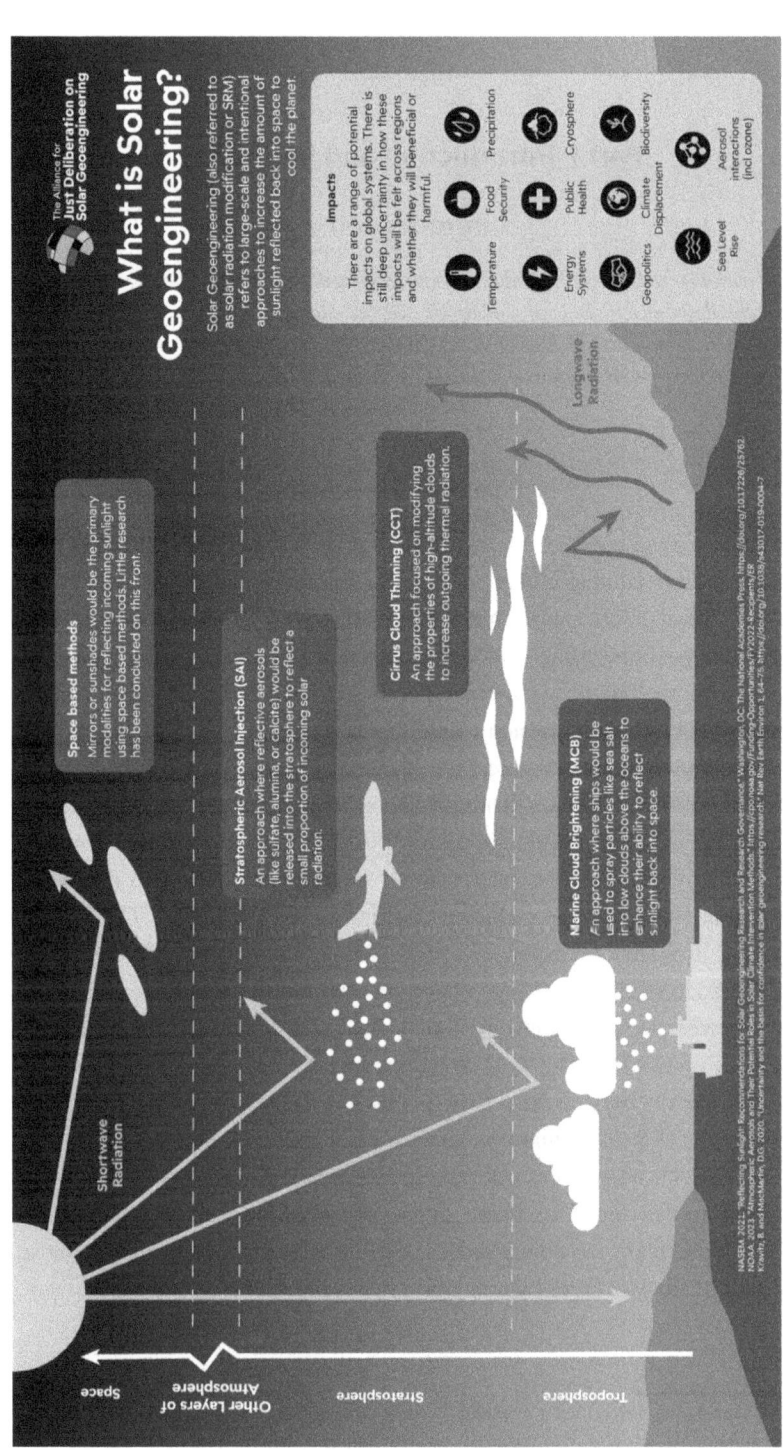

Figure 1 Overview of solar geoengineering methods. A larger version of the figure is avaialble to view online at www.cambridge.org/jinnah-et-al

Source: The Alliance for Just Deliberation on Solar Geoengineering.

offer three methods for how to do it, and provide briefing materials that can be adapted for use in a range of different public engagement contexts.[2]

Our primary contention is that in order for communities, publics, and other impacted groups to be meaningfully engaged in discussions and decision-making about SG, they must have sufficient capacity. Capacity is the information, skills, practices, and resources required to do something (Khan et al., 2018). In this case, those seeking to engage in discussion about SG must have access to information that enables them to understand, at a minimum, what SG is (Buck et al., 2025). As evidenced in recent attempts to develop governance mechanisms for SG and in recent multicountry survey research, publics lack familiarity and access to the foundational knowledge needed to develop positions on this topic (Baum et al., 2024; Dove et al., 2024a; DSG, 2023; Jinnah and Nicholson, 2019), and express desire for more information and education (Buck et al., 2025; Fritz et al., 2024). Where this capacity is insufficient, it must be built. Capacity building is therefore an essential prerequisite for engagement.

Capacity building is "a sustained process through which individuals, organizations, and societies mobilize and sustain knowledge, skills, tools, and practices that enable their ability to engage in and implement local, national, and international forms of ... governance" (DSG, 2023). Like public engagement, capacity building can come in many different forms. We are primarily interested in how those who seek to initiate public engagement – scientists and researchers, policymakers, practitioners, research funders, and others – can help participants build capacity to engage meaningfully in discussions and deliberations on SG and other emerging technologies.

We hope this Element will be used by people already thinking about the importance of public engagement surrounding emerging technologies, and/or who wish to provide public access to accurate and balanced information about SG and climate change. Importantly, we aim to support efforts to bring new voices into ongoing debates and discussions about SG and other emerging technologies.

Toward this end, we provide a comparative overview of three complementary methods that can be used to engage publics in discussions and governance around any emerging technology. The methods we selected are capacity building workshops, participatory technology assessment (pTA), and Deliberative Polling. In addition to drawing on the expertise of our team, we selected these methods to show how multiple methods can be used together or separately within a broader program to fill several identified engagement needs over time for different audiences and end users. Whereas capacity building workshops are most useful with civil society actors when emerging technologies are at their early stages,

---

[2] We are grateful to an anonymous reviewer for suggesting text in this and following paragraphs.

Deliberative Polling is more useful with policymakers when research and development are at a decision point, such as transitioning to field testing, choosing between deployment alternatives, or deciding whether to cease development altogether. The pTA approach is most useful somewhere in between with a plurality of audiences, when capacity is sufficient for informed discussion but public interests and concerns and ideas are yet underexplored or understood.

After presenting and discussing these methods, we drill down into SG specifically to showcase how briefing materials can be designed to build participants' engagement capacities across relevant scientific, political, and ethical issues. These materials are intended as a general model that can be adapted for use across a range of engagement methods – including, but not limited to the methods we discuss in this Element. Indeed, the briefing materials have already been utilized to prepare participants to engage in capacity building workshops facilitated by DSG. They could also be used to inform participants in pTA and Deliberative Polling. The Element is designed to be accessible to a broad set of users, including students, experts from diverse disciplines, policymakers, public engagement professionals, NGO practitioners, and others seeking a greater understanding of: SG's scientific, political, and ethical dimensions; and/or how to engage publics in research or discussion of SG and other emerging technologies.

Those thinking about how to build capacity for public engagement on other emerging technologies will find the Element useful. SG sits firmly at the intersection between cutting-edge scientific investigation, societal deliberation about appropriate responses to climate change, and widely divergent values about technological development and deployment. As such, this Element about SG is also about living in the messy and fast-moving world that faces tremendous challenges and opportunities. It should be of interest not just to people looking at SG, but to anyone concerned with how public engagement with science and emerging technologies of all kinds can best be facilitated. Most importantly, the SG focused briefing material we developed, and our envisioned process for updating and adapting the material as a living and collaborative project, provides a model that others can use to build capacity for public engagement on other emerging technologies and pressing issues.

A broad audience interested in other emerging technologies and issues can also take lessons from how we have addressed a key challenge that lies at the heart of our approach to building capacity for public engagement. On one hand, familiarity and awareness of SG across the world is low and recent research suggests many publics want more information and education on this issue (e.g., Baum et al., 2024; Fritz et al., 2024; Buck et al., 2025). On the other hand, information on SG is incomplete in several ways. First, although scientists and researchers from the Global South are increasingly involved in SG research, the existing knowledge base has been primarily built by scientists and researchers from a handful of countries in the Global North.[3] Second, the existing knowledge base on SG has also been driven by science as a way of producing knowledge about the world. Other relevant ways of knowing and producing knowledge, such as related to Indigenous knowledge, Traditional Ecological Knowledge (TEK), and place-based lay knowledge, have yet to be applied to the issue of SG. Therefore, as currently written, our briefing materials may not yet reflect the forms of knowledge, and the questions, issues, and concerns that may be of greatest importance to publics and communities outside of the Global North, especially those that may attach greater importance to forms of Indigenous or place-based knowledge.

This is a fundamental challenge that is likely to apply to many different emerging technologies, and is not unique to SG: People need to have access to existing knowledge about emerging technologies to contribute to and shape discussion; however, as ideas that originate within the minds of scientists and engineers, sometimes from particular parts of the world, early knowledge of emerging technologies will likely not reflect of all ways of knowing, nor will it likely address the concerns, questions, and salient issues for all communities. This is a primary reason why we think it is so important to expand the conversation on SG and other emerging technologies to publics and communities that have yet to be included.

We have developed one possible approach to addressing this challenge based on a dual process of updating the material to reflect evolving knowledge and adapting the material to fit local contexts. First, the authors will regularly update the core briefing materials in response to community feedback and developments in research and governance activity. We will host updated materials as well as feedback forms online at https://www.sikinajinnah.org/geoengineering-briefing-materials.html. Second, we encourage practitioners, researchers, and others that initiate engagement to use the updated materials as a model, and tailor and adapt the material to meet the information and format needs of specific audiences and local contexts. We have made this Element completely open access to facilitate that process. We therefore envision the briefing materials to be a living and collaborative project that evolves to incorporate community feedback and new information and knowledge, including knowledge generated through the engagement processes that we hope the materials help enable. Centrally, we offer these materials as a starting point for bringing new voices, perspectives, and forms of knowledge into discussion and research of SG.

---

[3] Our usage of the terms "Global South" and "Global North" is imperfect and we recognize that such broad terms lump together many heterogeneous and diverse societies and countries and obscures internal inequalities that create disparities in climate vulnerability within countries.

1.2 Why Solar Geoengineering?

SG provides a timely opportunity to model how and why public engagement can be designed to enhance participation and ultimately more just decision-making. SG is still relatively unknown by most members of the public, but that is set to change rapidly as climate impacts worsen, climate policies in key emitting states are rolled back, and (mis)information campaigns that target the media, the public, investors, governments, and intergovernmental bodies continue to grow. Proactively providing detailed, balanced, and evidence-based information in advance of important decisions about deployment and regulation of these technologies is therefore essential for democratic oversight of large-scale climate change adaptation and mitigation strategies.

We are motivated by the fact that too few people have a voice in conversations about SG and publicly accessible and digestible information about SG is limited to enable broader participation. This applies to many other emerging technologies as well. In this Element, we therefore provide a set of balanced and publicly accessible briefing materials about SG based on existing evidence that can be used to build capacity to enable various types of publics to engage in SG discussions. These materials are targeted to be accessible to the majority of English-speaking adult laypersons, following the guidelines of science agencies such as the US National Institutes of Health (National Institutes of Health, n.d.), and can be readily adapted and translated for various types of audiences, be it youth, policymakers, local community members, audiences in other countries, and so on.

1.3 The Importance of Public Engagement on Solar Geoengineering

The importance of public engagement in science, and more specifically in the research, development, and governance of emerging technologies, has been widely recognized by political (see, e.g., European Commission, 2002) and scientific authorities (see, e.g., NASEM, 2021; see also Potochnik and Jacquart, 2025). In the SG case, high-level and authoritative reports and assessments routinely call for some form of public engagement in research or governance (e.g., Chhetri et al., 2018; European Commission, 2024; NASEM, 2021; UNEP, 2023). The stated motivations for public engagement vary, but are often described in terms of instrumental, substantive, and normative rationales (Fiorino, 1990; Stirling, 2008). Earlier work has argued that all three motivations are relevant for SG and in fact engagement is necessary from ethical, political, and technological perspectives (Carr et al., 2013). The *normative* rationale recognizes that public engagement is simply the right thing to do, as affected populations deserve a say on matters that affect them. Public engagement may also aim to enhance justice, promote democracy, and fulfill ethical obligations (Hourdequin, 2019). On the assertion that technical experts and policymakers do not have a monopoly on relevant knowledge, the *substantive* rationale for public engagement is to improve SG research and decision-making through the integration of public knowledge and through robust deliberation between publics, experts, and policy-makers. This rationale aims to make SG research and governance *better* by engaging with diverse perspectives and by incorporating these into research, development, and governance processes. Instrumentally, public engagement aims to achieve predefined ends, such as enhance the legitimacy of SG research and build public trust in the researchers and institutions that produce and govern SG research. Other desired outcomes may include minimizing public opposition to SG research or development and raising public awareness. It may also include addressing inaccurate beliefs about SG, such as that governments are already using it, including by "inoculating" others from adopting these beliefs in the first place (Buck et al., 2025; Lewandowsky and van der Lindin, 2021). We know from other examples, such as nanotechnology, genetic engineering, and artificial intelligence, that public engagement, or at least perceived attempts at public engagement, can be critical to ensuring uptake of novel technologies.

Yet even as the study of SG, including limited real-world tests, is moving rapidly, publics around the world do not have strong awareness or understanding of this technology (Baum et al., 2024; Carlisle et al., 2020). Further, public engagement approaches have varied dramatically in the field. There is a growing trove of social science literature underscoring how critical engagement is for responsible research and innovation and principles of participatory justice (e.g., Carr et al., 2013; Corner et al., 2012; Grubert, 2024; Lavery, 2018; Low et al., 2022; NASEM, 2021; Scott-Buechler and Jinnah, 2024; Stilgoe et al., 2013a). Further, models exist to guide scientists and others on how to design and carry out public engagement for controversial emerging technologies to ensure it remains in the public interest (e.g., Jinnah et al., 2024; d'Angelo et al., 2021; O'Doherty and Einsiedel, 2013; Wilsdon and Willis, 2004). In the SG field, some early proposed field experiments, namely the United Kingdom's (SPICE) trial, embraced public engagement as part of an overall strategy to ensure the research was responsible and responsive to public values and concerns (Macnaghten and Owen, 2011; Pidgeon et al., 2013; Stilgoe et al., 2013b). However, others have eschewed public engagement. Some research teams have only announced field trials after they have already been initiated out of concern that critics would try to stop the trial (Flavelle and Bates, 2024). Others have assumed engagement wasn't necessary because proposed experiments lacked physical environmental impacts. In some of those cases, research teams – and those advising them – erroneously determined that normative and ethical concerns about technologies more broadly were insufficient to trigger public engagement needs (Jinnah et al., 2024a). In these cases, *failure* to engage publics yielded the precise impact that scientists feared engagement itself would lead to: the slowing and/or cancellation of their experiments.

1.4 Briefing Book Structure and Approach

Our briefing book contains five sections that cover different dimensions of SG and climate change, each of which is helpful to understand in order to develop an informed perspective on SG. Those sections address climate science, climate policy and responses, SG science, SG policy and governance, and SG ethics and justice. Each can be used independently or holistically, depending on audience and other engagement needs. The sections devoted to climate science and climate policy and responses can be used in more general climate change related engagements as well.[4] A preface to the briefing book clarifies the intended uses of the material, explains how we developed it, describes our vision for the material as a living and collaborative project, and discusses several issues to consider in adapting the material further to meet specific audience needs.

While our briefing materials are tailored to be accessible to English-speaking lay adults, different groups of people can have diverse and unique learning and accessibility needs. Additionally, as explained, different groups of people around the world may find certain issues, concerns, information, and questions more relevant than others. To enable effective capacity building, capacity building providers need to tailor information and communication to meet the specific needs of engaged audiences. Just as there is no one-size-fits-all solution to capacity building (Khan et al., 2018), there is no one-size-fits-all solution to providing broadly accessible information in support of capacity building efforts. We hope researchers and practitioners will use the materials to support their capacity building and engagement activities, including by adapting the material as needed.

We endeavor to present the information in the most accurate and balanced way possible. This is an incredibly challenging task, as the science is complex and characterized by deep uncertainties. Unlike other capacity building materials available for engagements on this topic, we therefore center expertise from the field of science communication. Two of our coauthors are experts in scientific communication and, prior to this project, had not worked on SG nor had any

---

[4] Those aiming to use the material for more general engagement on climate change should include expanded discussion of carbon dioxide removal and adaptation and potentially methane removal as response options. Our material currently includes only brief discussions of these options to save space for expanded discussion of SG.

preconceived opinions about it. Expertise in this field enables us to understand the evolving information landscape and tailor our materials according to emerging research about how to communicate science effectively (NASEM, 2017).

For instance, for many decades, science communication campaigns have employed a framework called the "deficit model" to try to influence the public to adopt evidence-based policies (NASEM, 2017; Wynne, 2006). According to the deficit model, members of the public adopt actions that are not supported by scientific evidence solely because they lack information about what "the science says" on issues such as vaccination, climate change policy, and genetic engineering. But recent research and real-world events, such as varying rates of COVID vaccination uptake among populations with differing political ideologies, have highlighted how this model fails to account for the many factors that influence people's decisions, including their values, sense of identity, attitudes about science and need for belonging to social groups (Potochnik and Jacquart, 2025). The deficit model also does not deal well with uncertainty, as it presupposes that scientific facts have already been established and that there is therefore a "right" or "wrong" decision to be made.

In contrast, effective science communication starts by understanding that different audiences have different interests, goals, values, and prior information about a particular topic. It requires science communicators to define the audience they are trying to reach and design their products accordingly (Hutchins, 2020).

Of course, the goal of public engagement should not be merely to transfer scientific knowledge to the public (Wynne, 2006). Rather, public engagement requires a multidirectional and deliberative exchange of information and knowledge between publics, other interested groups, and experts (Potochnik and Jacquart, 2025). Such an exchange would engage with – and respect – the knowledge, perspectives, values, and experiences already held by publics and interested groups. Our goal in providing the briefing material in Part 2 is therefore not simply to transfer knowledge to publics but rather to empower people to participate in SG discussion and governance by strengthening their capacity to understand – and contribute to our understanding of – SG and its scientific and social dimensions. In this view, effective science communication, alongside capacity building, is needed to enable robust and meaningful public engagement.

Drawing on the deep expertise of coauthor Erika Check Haden in science communication, we have used evidence-based practices to describe these issues in broadly accessible language to assist researchers and practitioners in adapting our materials to engage a variety of audiences. We therefore form a model for future large-scale public engagement on science projects in the realms of climate, public health, and beyond.

For instance, we have used techniques to improve readability of our briefing materials for general audiences, including eliminating jargon, writing shorter, more active sentences, using concrete subjects and verbs, and eliminating inessential information.

Additionally, most adults are not trained to calculate or interpret statistics and probabilities, or to read the types of complex figures and tables that normally accompany scientific texts. We have adapted our materials for audiences with varying numeracy levels by using comparisons to tangible objects to help readers contextualize critical statistics, probabilities, and numerical quantities.

Finally, the topic is not only complex but also controversial, and experts are split on many of the social, political, and ethical issues we explore in the briefing book. Fundamentally, experts have conflicting perspectives on how society should approach the prospect of SG. We have tried to cover these debates and disagreements through a fair and balanced presentation of the different positions and arguments that characterize much of the expert discussion on SG. We aim to allow our audience to evaluate the state of the evidence and arguments supporting various courses of action for themselves, to enable them to develop their own informed opinions on the topic.

1.5 Element Overview

The coauthors are agnostic on if SG should proceed or not. We are united, however, in the perspective that enabling more people to engage in that decision is essential for justice. Recalling Freeman Dyson's quote that opens this section: "whoever concerns [them]self with big technology, either to push it forward or to stop it, is gambling in human lives." Decisions about SG must involve far more people from more diverse geographies, ages, and other metrics of positionality. Those who wish to decide the fate of SG alone may end up with blood on their hands.

The Element is laid out as follows. Part I includes this introduction and Section 2, which presents three complementary methods for engaging publics in research governance about SG (and other technologies): capacity building workshops, participatory technology assessment (pTA), and Deliberative Polling. The methods can be used longitudinally within a broader program of engagement to address a range of engagement needs ranging from building foundational knowledge to informing specific points of decision-making.

Part II (Sections 3–8) contains the briefing materials, developed by all coauthors and peer-reviewed by leading experts in the field. Sections 3–8 use SG as a case to model how capacity building materials can be structured for broad engagement efforts. We hope this briefing book provides a template that can be used for developing materials for other emerging technologies. Part II

(Section 3) also provides more detailed information about how we hope these materials can be updated and improved over time and adapted for specific local contexts. We also have a companion website, which hosts materials for further learning and updated versions of the briefing materials (https://www.sikinajin nah.org/geoengineering-briefing-materials.html).

2 Methods for Engaging Publics

2.1 Introduction

There are a variety of methods that researchers and practitioners can use to engage publics and other interested groups on emerging technologies, including solar geoengineering (SG). In this section, we focus on three such methods - capacity building workshops, participatory technology assessment (pTA), and Deliberative Polling. These methods were selected based on the author's expertise to demonstrate how multiple complementary engagement methods can be used to build capacities across multiple sectors of society that enable informed public engagement in decision-making on SG and other emerging technologies. Importantly, each method is particularly well suited to different phases in the technological readiness spectrum and different audiences.

Each engagement method – including the ones we discuss here and others – carries strengths and limitations that make them potentially well-suited for some engagement purposes and likely poorly suited for others. No method is a one-size-fits-all solution. Rather, the three methods we selected are designed to address different sets of needs for different audiences that may arise through-out different stages of a technology's research and development trajectory, or different stages of a governance process. We selected these because they are complementary, in that each method can produce the conditions that enable the successful use of another method. Their use can be coordinated within a broader "program" of engagement to set the stage for meaningful public engagement on important decisions we may soon face. The methods are mutually reinforcing, and they address several related critical engagement needs for different audi-ences. These three methods cannot address all engagement needs, and these are also not the only available methods to choose from.

Our aim in showcasing the methods in this section is twofold. First, we aim to give readers an in-depth and structured exploration of several options for engagement methods from the perspectives of those with experience and expertise in using the methods. Second, we aim to show how the methods can relate to each other, and to demonstrate how using multiple methods in a broader program could enable more just and democratic decision-making on SG and other emerging technologies.

Specifically, we imagine a program that includes a sequential process whereby capacity building workshops build capacity that enables a successful pTA process, which can be used to guide a Deliberative Poll intended to inform specific policy-relevant decisions. First, capacity building workshops can help civil society organizations, policymakers, and experts build foundational knowledge about SG in the context of their own local, national, or regional circumstances and needs. Building this foundational knowledge is critical for the successful use of pTA, which requires local capacity and readiness to facilitate an assessment process that brings together groups that are underrepresented in scientific and technology assessment and decision-making, such as publics, interested groups, and affected communities. Foundational knowledge is also needed to enable impacted communities, interested groups, and experts to shape the issue framing, question selection, and engagement format of public forums within a pTA process. Among other possible purposes, pTA can then be used to understand public values surrounding potential courses of action and to explore social license for pursuing potential directions of research or development. This in turn is needed to inform which specific decisions and policy-options should be on the table for broad and inclusive public deliberation. Of the methods we discuss here, Deliberative Polling is then best positioned to facilitate broad public deliberation to inform specific policy-relevant decisions, such as whether to establish a research program or not, or to adopt a commitment to refrain from using SG or not. Other methods, such as public comment processes, would then be better positioned to integrate public views as needed on how decisions will be implemented, to enable publics to weigh in on, for example, how a regulatory framework for SG research will be designed. The successful implementation of those decisions in turn rests on policymakers, interested groups, and experts having the foundational knowledge and governance capacity that was generated through earlier capacity building workshops.

We begin with a discussion of capacity building workshops, as developed and carried out by coauthor Shuchi Talati and her colleagues at The Alliance for Just Deliberation on Solar Geoengineering (DSG). DSG and indeed all the coauthors see capacity building as foundational in the SG context in order to facilitate effective engagement work. We then turn to a discussion of participatory technology assessment (pTA) as developed by coauthor Mahmud Farooque and colleagues at Arizona State University. Finally, we discuss Deliberative Polling as led by coauthor Alice Siu at Stanford's Deliberative Democracy Lab. Table 1 provides an overview of these engagement methods and briefly outlines some of their key differences and commonalities.

Given our interest in including communities that are most vulnerable to climate change in the Global South in discussions and decision-making about

Table 1 Comparative overview of engagement methods

	Capacity building workshops	Participatory Technology Assessment (pTA)	Deliberative Polling
Aims and goals	Build participants' capacity to discuss, govern; empower participants to access and understand new knowledge	Varied: inform policy, decision-making; improve scientific literacy; map public values; engage underrepresented groups in scientific, technology assessment and decision-making	Understand what public opinion actually is; inform policy and decision-making; enhance democratic legitimacy
Who is engaged?	Variable: focus on civil society, policymaking, and academic sectors in climate vulnerable countries	Nonexpert societal groups: interested groups, publics, rightsholders, affected communities	Publics; any defined population
Who facilitates?	NGO with local partners (civil society, governments, academic groups)	Technology assessment agencies; network of academics, science educators	University research group, network of academics, experts, and policymakers
Key elements of method	Landscape analysis to understand geography; Modular workshops adapted to meet local needs; cocreation with long-term partners	Cocreation of issue framing and forum design; representative public deliberation forum; co-analysis of results and dissemination	Random, representative sampling; preliminary polling; creation of balanced briefing materials; small group deliberation; dialogue with experts; post-deliberation polling

SG, readers may be puzzled by our selection of engagement methods designed in the Global North. After all, the enduring wisdom is that methods that work in one context may not work in others, and to be most effective, methods must be tailored to resonate with regional, national, or local sociopolitical contexts (e.g., Busch et al., 2025; Carr et al., 2013). Indeed, there are many diverse cultures within and across countries in the Global South, some of which may have diverse understandings of and approaches to, for example, democracy, representation, agency, truth and knowledge, and public involvement in decision-making. However, following DSG's capacity building model, we do not assume that all cultures have understandings of these issues that diverge from Western contexts, and we emphasize the responsibility of engagement initiators and practitioners in working with local partners to understand local contexts so that decisions to tailor methods can be made on a case by case basis.

We think our discussion of these methods should be of interest to a broad readership for two reasons. First, readers can consider how key aspects of these methods may or may not apply in the contexts they are interested in, and how broader programs of engagement can include multiple complementary methods. Second, we also suggest that, with some modifications and tailoring, these methods *can* be led by Global South actors, and so should not be dismissed out of hand.

First and foremost, although it was designed in the United States, Deliberative Polling has been used successfully in many diverse geographic and cultural contexts around the world, including dozens of times across South America, Africa, and Asia (see e.g., Fishkin et al., 2017). Participant evaluation of these events is consistently positive. For example, 84 percent of participants in a Deliberative Polling in Brazil in 2009 thought the process was valuable, and 53 percent indicated it was "extremely valuable."[5] Additionally, DSG's capacity building program is inspired by a model of capacity building that originates from the Global South, as articulated by researchers, policymakers, and practitioners involved in the Least Developed Country (LDC) Initiative for Effective Adaptation and Resilience (LIFE-AR) and the UNFCCC Capacity Building Framework (DSG, 2023; Khan et al., 2018; LIFE-AR, 2019). DSG, launched in 2023, has thus far run multiple capacity building workshops in partnership with local organizations in different countries across South Asia, Southern Africa, and Latin America. Finally, pTA is based on the World Wide Views (WWViews) model of global citizen consultations which was used to inform negotiations under the UN Convention on Biological Diversity and the UN Framework Convention for Climate Change (Worthington et al., 2012b). The method could also be applied in different parts of the world if certain conditions are met, as we discuss next. Overall, a quick survey of public participatory processes and innovations in deliberative democracy in the Global South, for example, in Latin America, suggests that approaches to

---

[5] Secretary-General, Rio Grande do Sul State Government. 2009. 1st Deliberative Polling in Rio Grande do Sul State – Executive Summary. https://deliberation.stanford.edu/news/final-report-1st-deliberative-pollingr-rio-grande-do-sul-state-public-servants-career-reform.

engagement and deliberation in this context share both differences and similarities to the methods we discuss here (Pogrebinschi and Ross, 2019). While the methods have relevance beyond the context of the United States and Europe, they may need to be tailored and adapted to be effective in other sociopolitical contexts.[6] Therefore, we also discuss whether and how these methods may need to be tailored to meaningfully engage communities in different contexts. Others have provided helpful guidance for engaging specific climate vulnerable communities, such as Busch et al. (2025) who identify several types of engagement models that can be "used to progress Indigenous-inclusive engagement across Canadian Indigenous communities" on SG (p. 4).

Given our focus on building capacity for public engagement, it's important to note that these and other methods of engagement have a multifaceted relationship with capacity building. As explained in Section 1, capacity building is needed to enable these methods, in part to ensure that engagement is meaningful, which requires that participants have capacity to participate in the activities and shape any outcomes on an equitable basis. But these methods can also build the capacities of the individuals and groups that participate. By participating in the deliberation, assessment, learning, and other activities and processes within each method, participants develop vital skills, competencies, and practices that enable them to be more informed and effective participants in SG discussion and decision-making. Capacity building is therefore both a prerequisite and an outcome of these methods, and of engagement with publics and other interested groups more broadly.

2.2 Capacity Building Workshops

2.2.1 Aims and Purpose

The term "capacity building" is imprecise. There is no established or agreed upon definition, which results in a diverse and wide set of activities (Dove et al., 2024a). Organizations and institutions have been doing different types of capacity building on climate, environment and development for several decades now, and in that time, there have been significant learnings about what works and what doesn't work. In the "classic" capacity building model, outside consultants, typically from private consulting firms in Global North countries, are brought into recipient

---

[6] See, e.g., the LATINNO project documenting participatory processes in Latin America: www .latinno.net/en/. We are aware of ongoing discussion surrounding the need to learn from experience and innovations in engagement, participation, and deliberative democracy in the Global South. Our focus on methods designed in the Global North is not intended to discount this need. See, e.g., https://deliberativehub.wordpress.com/2023/04/02/learning-from-participation-and-deliberation-in-the-global-south/; https://www.publicdeliberation.net/resisting-colonisation-avoiding-tropicali sation-deliberative-wave-in-the-global-south/; www.idea.int/news/climate-deliberation-global-south

countries on a short-term basis to train personnel. This dominant approach to capacity building is commonly critiqued as short-term, projectized and sectoral, and led by many different donors, some with deep bias, with little coordination between them and without sufficient ownership on behalf of targeted countries or communities (Casado Asensio et al., 2022; Eade, 2007; Khan et al., 2018).

In contrast, the model discussed here is one that the Alliance for Just Deliberation on Solar Geoengineering (DSG) is trying to implement and is inspired by recent efforts to rethink this approach to capacity building. These efforts have culminated in the creation of a new capacity building model that improves upon common critiques and limitations of the classic model. This model aims to build long-term, durable, and sustainable capacity systems that enable countries to effectively address issues and solve goals over time. At the core of this approach are capacity building workshops based on unbiased information, cocreation, and long-term partnerships with a potential range of local actors from civil society that understand the context and needs and that can be focal points for sustaining and strengthening governance capacity long into the future. Multiple local partners in one region can also address different groups and sectors across civil society (e.g., think tanks, advocacy, or community based organizations) to reach a wider audience.

The ultimate goal of any capacity building program should be to empower participants to have access to and understand new areas of knowledge. Very little knowledge on SG exists, and without approaches that center unbiased and sustained knowledge, biased narratives will fill the vacuum. DSG's goals are to democratize knowledge in climate vulnerable communities and countries, and ultimately elevate voices in these regions to develop and represent their perspectives in decision-making spaces. These are the populations that are most vulnerable to both climate change and SG, and the most to gain or lose from decision-making in the SG space. This is designed in the context of anticolonial politics, which dictate that these communities and countries from the Global South are able to and empowered to engage in questions around whether and how SG should proceed (DSG, 2023).

The target sectors of these workshops are largely civil society, policy-makers, and academia. Civil society is specifically important as it functions as an arena for societal deliberation, comprised of "a network of groups, communities, and voluntary associations that is distinct from the state and that excludes profit-motivated entities," such as policy research organizations, advocacy organizations, and community-based groups (DSG, 2023; Edwards, 2011). DSG prioritizes this sector for three overarching reasons :

> (1) Whereas states have been reluctant to take steps to govern solar geoengineering, civil society can play constructive roles in establishing

inclusive and just forms of governance in the near future. (2) Civil society can act as a conduit for diverse communities and groups to engage in solar geoengineering governance, thereby broadening the diversity of perspectives, values, and worldviews that are included in deliberations and considered in decisions. (3) Governments and political institutions can be volatile, which can undermine the dedicated and consistent efforts needed to govern solar geoengineering over long time periods if left to states alone. (DSG, 2023)

Building off these goals and priorities, DSG developed overarching principles and high-level objectives to guide this work, listed in Table 2. These were built based on ideas and knowledge from "the capacity building literature, initiatives from the Least Developed Countries (LDC) Group including the LDC Initiative for Effective Adaptation and Resilience (LIFE-AR), and the UNFCCC Capacity Building Framework" (DSG, 2023; Khan et al., 2018; LIFE-AR, 2019).

Table 2 Overarching principles and objectives of modernized capacity building workshops

Principle/objective	Description
Cocreate with local partners	Cocreate with regional and community partners to lead the way in identifying capacity needs and designing capacity building projects and outcomes.
Center local context and innovation	Successful capacity building will look different in different places and that have different capacity needs. Work with local partners to develop deliberative methods that are best suited for local communities, including those that are unaccustomed to traditional methods involving printed text and lectures.
Build off of what is already there	Work with partners to identify forms of capacity that exist so we can build off of what our local partners already do well.
Be holistic	A wide breadth of skills and capacity among a wide range of actors is required to govern SG, and we build capacities that are often taken-for-granted and less tangible and visible.
Foster Collaboration	Partner and coordinate with other organizations working on SG and related areas of capacity building to ensure our efforts align.

Table 2 (cont.)

Principle/objective	Description
Prioritize procedural justice	Do not have biases around whether our local partners decide to support or oppose SG research or potential deployment; we believe that they should have the opportunity to form their own positions and, critically, be able to engage when these decisions are made.
Be anticipatory	Anticipate evolving trends in SG research to ensure that our capacity building prepares local partners to respond to current developments.
Embrace modulatory	Develop modular learning and projects that can be deployed in different arrangements and adapted to local contexts to make it easier for our capacity building efforts to reach as many people as possible over a short period of time.
Value diverse forms of knowledge	Local partners can develop the most complete understanding of SG and its implications by integrating science with other relevant ways of knowing, such as traditional ecological knowledge.
Foster self-reflection and assessment	Continuously assess and improve how we do capacity building. We also have forms of capacity that need to be built and strengthened, such as the ability to understand local contexts and to provide education and training in the most effective ways possible.
Ensure sustainability	Ensure that partners or processes are in place to continue capacity building work that (1) enables participants to utilize knowledge and (2) reaches new participants.

2.2.2 Origins, Broader Context, and Current State of Use

DSG was launched as a nonprofit organization in April 2023 to implement this model of work. It is in early stages of being able to evaluate its success as it moves through different phases. This model of work is inherently slow, centered on trust and long-term processes.

These capacity building workshops are not a novel approach but an attempt to utilize recommendations for updating traditional capacity building methods in climate intervention for the needs and outcomes outlined earlier. There are other efforts in parallel fields that utilize different aspects of the updated approach that DSG is also attempting.

As mentioned, previous capacity building scholarship outlines two broad models of implementation (Khan et al., 2018). An older, "classic" model describes previous forms of capacity building, which are largely uncoordinated, ad hoc, unsustained, and led by external/nonlocal consultants for training. A "new" model aims to move beyond these limitations to be more innovative, sustainable, and locally owned (Dove et al., 2024a). These models are not limited to climate intervention or even climate broadly; they are expansive across fields. The latter, "new" model is what DSG attempts to build off of, which is an iterative approach that aims to continuously learn from itself and improve to achieve the goals described.

2.2.3 Methodology

The critical initial steps of this approach are understanding potential (1) geographies, (2) partners, and (3) participants to be the leaders and members of a capacity building process. Identifying these regions and actors requires a collaborative and thoughtful analysis of the landscape on the ground, including scientific, policy, and political considerations. There are major potential challenges in each of these key steps, limited by access, connections, and willingness to engage in a controversial field.

Geographies: Determining locations of engagement is a complex process, determined by both quantitative and qualitative metrics (DSG, 2024). Further landscape analysis to understand the range of potential stakeholders requires analytical research and conversations with experts and stakeholders on the ground, resulting in a set of organizations and experts that merit further discussion and engagement.

Partners: Narrowing down potential partners is not a one-off, but can happen at multiple different stages as engagement and capacity building continue via different mechanisms. Multiple local partners in one region can also help address different sets of participants across communities or sectors. However, initial dedicated engagement on the ground in a particular country and community, based on the regional analysis earlier, is necessary. The goals of this process are to start (1) learning how current organizations and experts are thinking about both SG, if at all, as well as efforts around capacity building for civil society; (2) exploring ways that a new organization like DSG can be supportive of locally driven initiatives and efforts to grow policy capacity in civil society; and (3) building the groundwork for partnerships and collaborations through which DSG can help catalyze work. Identifying partners subsequently enables a cocreated process through which they can suggest a range of potential capacity building mechanisms (e.g., workshops to different ends) that DSG can colead with additional resources (time, expertise, and funding).

Participants: Identifying participants is a coled process with DSG and its partner. These participants will be determined by the expertise of the partner, the capacity building mechanism, and the goal of a particular capacity building project. Participants can vary across sectors (e.g., civil society, academia, policymakers, private sector), communities, and perspectives.

In designing a capacity building workshop, our method is also focused on modularity to be able to tailor the design to the needs of a partner and participants. Different levels of understanding, familiarity, and interest will depend on their needs, desires, and roles. This includes, but is not limited to the scientific understanding of climate change and SG as well as a foundational understanding of climate and SG governance and its history.

2.2.4 Strengths and Limitations

Each method discussed in this Element is best suited to accomplish different outcomes. The outcomes of these capacity building workshops are to increase the participation of civil society and policymakers for future governance of SG. This moves beyond building the general knowledge of broad publics and understanding preferences. There are several advantages to this focus:

- The potential to reach a cross section of mission-driven organizations (including climate, energy environment, human rights, democracy, and other types of focus) as well as categories of organizations (advocacy, think tanks, community-based, etc.).
- The ability to have sustained engagement with partners and participants with expertise that may be motivated to be engaged in the field.
- The capacity to provide direct input into governance and decision-making processes.

The main disadvantage of this approach is an inability to reach lay audiences and nonexpert publics to build high-level understanding about SG and subsequently understand public perception. These workshops should therefore not be used to elicit public perspectives to inform specific points of decision-making. However, workshops have inherent limitations in the audiences they can reach. This method is focused on trying to enable a deeper impact on outcomes and decision-making in SG from this format.

2.2.5 Broader Implications

The potential of this method to strengthen the relationship between SG science, governance, and democracy will ultimately depend on who is willing to participate, the interest and dedication of local partners, and their choices around continued engagement in the field. Importantly, it will also be deeply dependent on the funding available to conduct such work, which remains deeply limited.

Democracy and public engagement require an informed set of participants, and this approach attempts to fulfil this important criteria to achieving legitimate outcomes. Building not only access to knowledge, but mechanisms to build upon it and use it are absolutely critical to changing the paradigm around the limited discussions on "public acceptance" and "social license" that we see for climate intervention technologies today.

2.3 Participatory Technology Assessment

Participatory technology assessment (pTA) refers to a group of methods and systematic procedures to involve "societal groups – stakeholders, affected citizens, nonexperts, and the public in general – in assessing technology and its consequences" (Grunwald, 2018). An explicit aim of pTA is to engage groups of nonexperts who are representative of the general population but who – unlike political, academic, industry, nongovernment, and advocacy organizations – are generally underrepresented if not absent in science and technology-related discourse and decision-making. The multilayered engagement process involves creating systematic communication and dialogue processes within and among groups, from affected people and communities to stakeholders, rightsholders, and the broader public (Figure 2).

2.3.1 Aims and Purpose

The objective of pTA can be varied: from filling democratic gaps and contributing to public dialogues to enriching policy advice and supporting institutional transformations (Grunwald, 2018). To date, federal and philanthropic sponsors have supported ECAST pTA projects for four specific objectives: (a) informing policy and decision-making (planetary defense), (b) improving scientific literacy (community climate hazards), (c) mapping public values (human gene editing), and (d) innovating public engagement (nuclear waste siting).

Specific to SG, objectives for conducting a pTA process can be fourfold: (a) providing social appraisals, (b) mapping public values, (c) filling representation gaps, and (d) integrating living and lived knowledge. Upstream SG governance poses a classic post-normal science (PNS) challenge characterized by high socio technical uncertainties, value conflicts, and urgent decision stakes (Bellamy et al., 2012; Funtowicz and Ravetz, 1993). Social appraisal of SG research, testing, and deployment needs to be undertaken at technology governance relevant scales, often at the same time as their expert appraisals. Second, empirical social science research on public values of SG is limited to a few

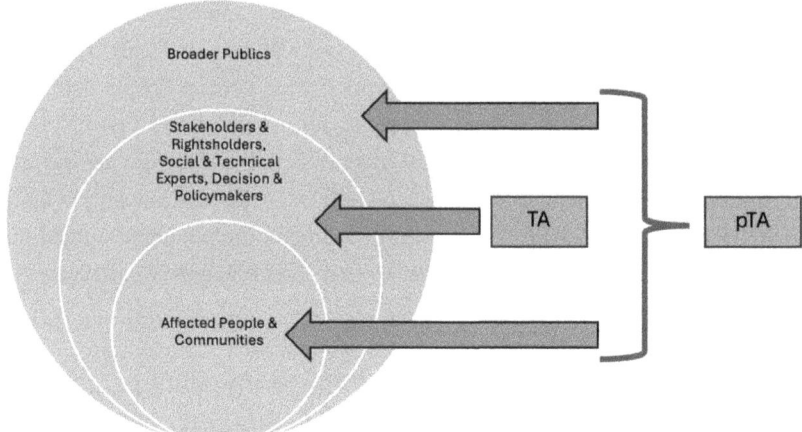

Figure 2 Publics, technology assessment (TA), and participatory technology assessment (pTA)

Source: Used with permission of The National Academies Press, from Gene Drives on the Horizon: Advancing Science, Navigating Uncertainty, and Aligning Research with Public Values, by the National Academies of Sciences, Engineering, and Medicine, 2016; permission conveyed through Copyright Clearance Center, Inc. This content is licensed by Taylor & The National Academies Press, and is NOT part of the Gold Open Access license. Definitions of community, stakeholder, and public expanded by the author with arrows to illustrate the differences and overlap between technology assessment and participatory technology assessment.

applications and a focus on countries in the Global North (Burns et al., 2016; Dove et al., 2024b). More dialogic research is needed to map public values and connect them to SG decisions and policymaking. Third, pTA can systematically engage those commonly missing in expert SG discourse. By including these voices in the SG policy and decision-making process, pTA can lead to more inclusive, useful, effective, fair, just, and equitable outcomes.

For example, in 2017, ECAST conducted a PTA process to map public values on SG research and democratic governance (Kaplan et al., 2019). It was precipitated by funding, governance, and scaling challenges faced by a few SG research initiatives. With support from the Sloan Foundation, ECAST worked collaboratively with scientists, funders, advisory bodies, and advocacy organizations to conduct the pTA. Representatively diverse groups of participants in Boston and Phoenix were engaged in informed and inclusive day-long facilitated deliberations on ethical issues (moral hazard, technological lock-ins, uncertainty, etc.; see the SG ethics and justice discussion in Section 8), types of geoengineering (SAI, MCB, etc.; see the SG science discussion in Section 6), scale and direction (small field experiments, coordinated acceleration, etc.), funding (public, private, philanthropic, etc.) and research governance (self-governance, advisory bodies, international negotiations, etc.) preferences. Results from the pTA were shared widely with scientists, funders, and decision-makers involved in various aspects of SG research. Materials created to facilitate the pTA process were used to engage other stakeholders and broaden the societal discourse.

2.3.2 Origins, Background, Current State of Use

Participatory technology assessment originated in Western Europe during the 1980s as a response to social movements around demands for peace, sustainability, and more deliberative democracy by technology assessment (TA) agencies, such as the Danish Board of Technology (DBT) and the Rathenau Institute (Grunwald, 2018; Joss and Belucchi, 2002). TA agencies are organized bodies dedicated to providing expert policy advice through systemic assessment of emerging issues in science and technology. Inspired by the founding of the US Congressional Office of Technology Assessment (OTA) in 1972, many European countries began establishing their own TA agencies from the mid-1980s and onward. In addition to strong analytical capacities, some of the agencies introduced innovative methods for citizen participation in their assessment processes (Worthington et al., 2012a). In the United States, Loka Institute was among the early proponents of pTA, particularly following the defunding of OTA in 1995 and subsequent efforts for revival (Guston, 2023). During the mid-2000s, public engagement in science (PES) in general and pTA in particular experienced a period of renewed interest and rapid growth through the US government's support of the Nanoscale Informal Science Education Network (NISENet), coled by the Boston Museum of Science (MOS) and Centers for Nanotechnology and Society (CNS), coled by the Consortium for Science, Policy and Outcomes (CSPO) at the Arizona State University.

In 2010, Loka, CSPO, and MOS joined the Science and Technology Innovation Program at the Woodrow Wilson Center and the citizen science platform SciStarter to launch the Expert and Citizen Assessment of Science and Technology (ECAST) Network to develop a pTA capacity in the United States building on European achievements. ECAST combined nonpartisan policy analysis, social assessments of emerging technologies, and informal science education and public engagement. Its goals included continually innovating concepts and practices and integrating the outcomes in policymaking, technological research and development (R&D), and wider societal deliberations (Sclove, 2010).

A pilot global citizen consultation project with DBT to inform the 2012 UN Convention on Biological Diversity paved the way for ECAST's project with

NASA on its Asteroid Initiative, a first for a US federal agency. In the decade that followed, through innovative applications in a variety of areas (i.e., community resilience, nuclear waste management, climate change, driverless car, and human gene editing) ECAST developed a reflexive, adaptable, and scalable three-phase model of pTA that could be applied at the local, national and global levels (Kaplan et al., 2021). ECAST pTA methodology has been cited in governmental reports on open innovation (GAO, 2016), methods to assess equity (OMB, 2021), and federal policy for public engagement (PCAST, 2023). Notable contributions to date include the planetary defense coordination office at NASA (Farooque and Kessler, 2023), environmental literacy theory of change at the National Oceanic and Atmospheric Administration (NOAA), and shared principles for community collaboration at the Department of Energy (DOE).

2.3.3 Methodology

ECAST pTA unfolds in three phases (Kaplan et al., 2021; Figure 3). First, a balanced problem framing is achieved by engaging subject matter experts, stakeholders, and community members (Issue Framing and Design). Public deliberations, the second step, engage diverse public members on potential options or considerations for research and development in one or more locations. The third phase is results integration. Decision-makers and other intended users interpret deliberative forums' qualitative and quantitative results and help integrate those findings with research, decision-making, and other types of engagement. Participatory technology assessment is a layered and iterative engagement process between members of the community (specific groups of interest or people directly impacted), stakeholders (experts, funders, regulators, professionals, advocates, and organized interests), and the public (broader democratic voting population). We elaborate on each phase next.

Phase I: Issue Framing and Design

Phase I of a pTA project utilizes a combination of (a) literature review, (b) stakeholder interviews, and (c) open-frame community dialogues to inform a (d) forum design workshop with experts and stakeholders. The details and extent of each are codeveloped in consultation and cooperation with the project sponsor, target audience, relevant experts, and stakeholders. A review of existing data, statistics, materials, and literature is conducted to understand the underlying science, technology, and societal issues and develop a preliminary expert-stakeholder value map to guide engagement activities such as stakeholder interviews, community dialogues, and forum design workshops.

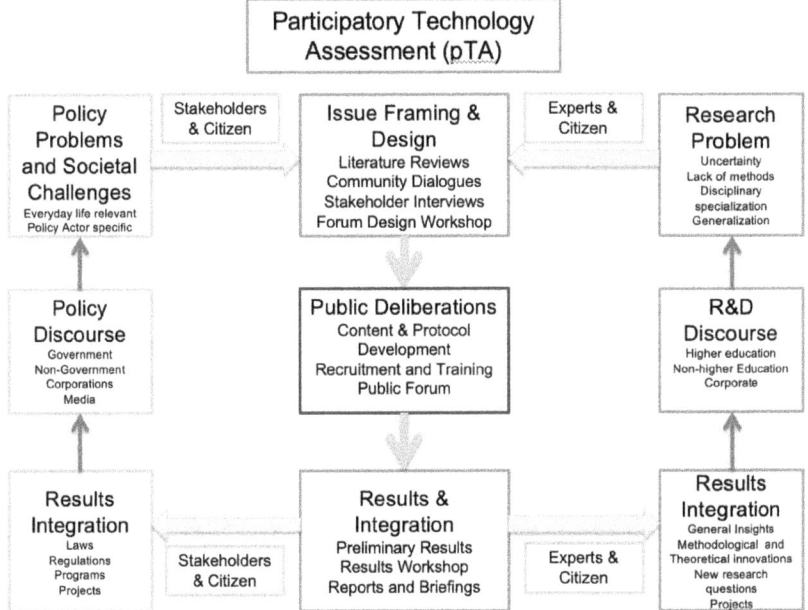

Figure 3 Three-phase pTA process The ECAST engagement model superimposed on a conceptual model for an ideal transdisciplinary process by author.

Source: Adapted from Figure 1 in D. J. A. Lang, M. Wiek, M. Bergmann, P. Stauffacher, P. Martens, P. Moll, M. Swilling, and C. J. Thomas, "Transdisciplinary Research in Sustainability Science: Practice, Principles, and Challenges," *Sustainability Science* 7, no. 1 (2012): 25–43. This content is licensed by Springer Nature Customer Service Center GmbH, and is NOT part of the Gold Open Access license. Springer Nature has provided permission to reproduce this material.

Community dialogues usually engage 12–15 participants over two 4-hour sessions. They are motivated by two recognitions. First, public concerns may only sometimes align with those of experts, and an expert-designed series of questions can miss latent issues important to the public. Second, people directly impacted by a proposed field experiment, demonstration project, or mass deployment have unique experiences and perspectives that may differ from the broader democratic public. The community dialogues thus begin with an "open frame" designed to meet the participants where they are rather than where the experts would like them to be. They seek to elicit both open-ended general hopes and concerns about their communities and the science and technology issues of interest.

The forum design workshop convenes 20–25 diverse subject matter experts and stakeholders over 1 ½ to 2 days to discuss and review the literature review outcomes, stakeholder interviews, and community dialogues. It has two objectives. First, to guide the topics, questions, content, participants, and useful outcomes of the public forums. Second, to help populate a balanced expert panel to review the deliberation materials, protocols, and preliminary results. Workshop participants are engaged through lightning talks, small and large group discussions about technological opportunities and uncertainties, societal implications, governance options, and deliberation design.

Phase II: Public Deliberations

The second phase of a PTA project entails (a) the design and development of content and protocols for the public forums, (b) the selection of forum locations, partners, and target public participants, and (c) the convening of deliberations in one or more geographies of interest.

Public deliberation forums are structured, informed, and facilitated day-long deliberations among a group of lay participants selected through an open application process to represent diversity in demography, ideology, and lived experiences relevant to the topic. Four criteria guide the design choices for the forums: diverse representation, informed participants, deliberative multidirectional learning, and transparent, comparable, and usable outputs and outcomes. Between 80 and 100 lay participants are recruited through an open application process to be representative of the diversity of the geographic areas of interest and provided a flat stipend for their participation. All participants receive informational briefing packets featuring the technical aspects, salient issues, questions, and areas of uncertainty related to the topic a week before the deliberation.

The forum day is usually divided into thematic discussion sessions. Participants sit in groups of 5–6 and are guided by a trained lead and group facilitators. Each session includes a presentation of background information, usually through a short video, a facilitated group discussion involving materials such as cards, boards, and workbooks, and a mediated question and answer period with subject matter experts. At the end of each session, participants provide individual and group responses to deliberation prompts and questions.

A detailed minute-by-minute facilitation protocol is developed to train group facilitators, support staff, and optional note-takers. A parallel data collection protocol is designed to match the pTA objectives. In addition to the participants' demographic data and written responses, the protocol may include pre and post surveys, table observations, and post-forum interviews of participants and facilitators.

Phase III: Results and Integration

The final phase of the pTA uses a series of post-deliberation activities, including (a) preliminary analysis, (b) results workshop, and (c) reports and briefings to inform and integrate the pTA outputs and outcomes into research, policy, education, and stimulate broader societal engagement. A multisite pTA process generates voluminous quantitative and qualitative data on public values collected through individual written rationales, group written rationales, table observer notes, audio recordings, and transcriptions. A preliminary analysis is conducted based on the review and guidance of the external reviewers for presentation at the results workshop.

Results and Integration Workshop convenes 20–25 diverse experts and stakeholders, usually for a day, many of whom participated in the forum design workshop. The objectives are to (a) review the preliminary results, (b) provide feedback and guidance about interesting and relevant findings, (c) identify areas for deeper analysis, and (d) recommend opportunities for sharing them with different audience groups.

The guidance and recommendations received at the results workshop are used to conduct detailed analyses using qualitative social science methods. These analyses generate reports, briefings, policy memos, and other publications for different target audience groups. Learning and engagement materials are distributed to engage public audiences at schools, libraries, and museums.

2.3.4 Strengths and Limitations

Built on DBT's World Wide Views (WWViews) model of global citizen consultations (Worthington et al., 2012b), the three-phase pTA methodology (Kaplan et al., 2021) is an established, evidence-based and relatively inexpensive, reflexive, adaptable, and scalable public engagement methodology. It can assess public values, help manage sociotechnical uncertainties, integrate living and lived knowledge, and bridge democratic gaps in SG research and governance. DBT developed WWViews as a "cheap and easy" (Worthington et al., 2012) public participation method for informing UN negotiations.

The model offers economies of scale. For example, ECAST's public engagement project on community resilience to climate hazards was piloted at eight museums with a US$500,000 budget. A similarly sized grant helped expand it to twenty-eight museums in the subsequent funding cycle. The three-phase model is flexible. It can be applied as a whole or in parts for different objectives. It is adaptable. The model can be adjusted and calibrated to meet changing public value priorities such as equity and procedural, distributive, intergenerational, and distributive justice. The three-phase PTA's adaptability extends to other deliberative approaches, such as consensus conferences, citizen juries, or citizen assemblies, which can be applied sequentially (substituting phase II) or in parallel. The Global Citizen Assembly project on gene editing was designed to leverage the ECAST pTA project on human gene editing in the United States and citizen jury projects in Australia and other countries (Dryzek et al., 2020).

The adaptability feature and distributed nature of the three-phase pTA methodology, while a strength in its recent growth in application, is also a limitation in terms of standardization, scaling, and diffusion. Much burden is placed on a small team of experienced practitioners to maintain, add, and apply the lessons learned across different application contexts and domains. Moreover, while pTA excels at gauging social perspectives on whether and how to pursue research or development of certain technologies, it should not be used to make specific decisions in isolation, for example, to allow an outdoor experiment to proceed or not. A successful pTA process also requires informed expert and civil society groups and project partners to help design and host the process, so it is most effective when local organizational infrastructure for engagement is available.

2.3.5 Broader Implications

Since its launch in 2010, ECAST has successfully socialized the three-phase methodology within the United States through opportunistic and continuous innovations one project at a time while maintaining active collaborations with European efforts. Within Western democracies, its two principal challenges are (a) institutionalization and (b) scaling the current efforts to be functional from the community scale to the regional and global scales. While daunting, a solution can come through two near-term interventions. First, within governments, a dedicated unit could be established focused specifically on pTA implementation, training, and capacity building (Weller et al., 2025). To complement and empower the mission of the governmental pTA units, a dedicated research unit focused on experimentation, evaluation, integration, and best practices on SG and other climate intervention technology applications could be established. In other contexts, pTA could be used if funding is available and local partners and interested groups are ready to support a pTA process for one or more of the four suitable objectives.

2.4 Deliberative Polling

Conventional opinion polling are traditional methods of measuring public opinion on various issues, policies, or candidates through structured surveys conducted with a representative sample of the population (Bradburn et al., 2004). These polls rely on established methodologies, including random or stratified sampling, to ensure diverse and accurate representation. The questions are generally carefully designed to minimize bias and often include multiple-choice or scaled responses. While these polls provide valuable snapshots of public sentiment and track trends over time, they are not without limitations. Challenges like nonresponse bias, the influence of question wording, and high costs can affect their accuracy and efficiency (Prosser and Mellon, 2018). As such, the method of Deliberative Polling has become an innovative way of gathering the public's opinion to provide a more in-depth understanding of what the people would think if they were informed (Mansbridge, 2010). The method of Deliberative Polling presents an opportunity for the public to engage with their fellow participants to learn and discuss important policy issues together.

2.4.1 Aims and Purpose

The method of Deliberative Polling aims to bring to light what "would" people think if they had the opportunity to engage in discussions with diverse others with vetted briefing materials and time to pose questions to balanced panels of experts and policymakers (Fishkin, 2009). Conventional ways of gathering the public only captures "what" people are thinking, and often "what" people are thinking come merely from soundbites and headlines (Fishkin, 2009).

The aim of Deliberative Polling is to overcome three major problems with conventional public opinion polling (Fishkin, 2009). First, rational ignorance. This concept refers to making a conscious choice to avoid learning something because the effort of gaining that knowledge is simply not worth the time (Downs, 1957). It implies that, in some cases, it can be entirely reasonable to opt for staying uninformed. For example, many argue that any given voter only has one vote, and therefore, what real impact can one single vote have on the outcome of an election? According to this perspective, the time and effort spent voting, let alone researching who or what to vote for, is simply not worth the benefit of making a slightly more informed vote.

Second, phantom opinions. This concept refers to people giving answers to questions even though they really don't have an answer. The best example of phantom opinions is the survey experiment run by George Bishop regarding the Public Affairs Act of 1975 (Bishop et al., 1980). The punchline is this Act doesn't exist. But, the survey results showed respondents offered their opinions to a fictitious Act. Put simply, respondents lied about knowing and having an opinion about this Act. These two problems of rational ignorance and phantom opinions call into question just how reliable conventional public opinion polls are, when the public often choose not to pay attention to politics and policies and, worse, will lie about their knowledge when asked.

And, third, communication with the like-minded. Through technology, the ability to *only* see the information we want to see, communicate with people we want to communicate with, and block out any information or people we don't want, has placed individuals into their own silos and many have argued that these technologies have made individuals in our society more polarized and extreme as a result (Kubin and von Sikorski, 2021; Sunstein, 2017).

These three problems – rationally choosing to not engage in politics, lying about knowing or having opinions toward politics, and being in information silos – are making it more and more difficult to understand how people think about pressing issues. Because conventional surveys are unable to provide reliable information, the method of Deliberative Polling serves to fill this void (Fishkin, 2009). Deliberative Polling not only provides participants the opportunity to engage with diverse others in conversation, but does so where participants have access to the same set of balanced and vetted materials, so that there is a basis of discussion. The purpose of Deliberative Polling is to provide the space for participants to form considered opinions. When doing so not only do participants become more informed and thoughtful, but they also walk away with the skills necessary to continue engaging with those that may disagree with them (Fishkin et al., 2021).

2.4.2 Origins, Background, Current State of Use

The method of Deliberative Polling was developed by James Fishkin in 1988. Fishkin saw the limitations of conventional public opinion and wanted to design a method that would pave the path for a more informed public. Deliberative Polling is a registered trademark of James Fishkin to ensure the quality and consistency of the methodology during implementation. Any funds generated from the trademark are used for research for the Stanford Deliberative Democracy Lab.

As of 2024, Deliberative Polling has been conducted in more than 50 countries, implemented over 150 projects. The method of Deliberative Polling has had significant policy impact in numerous countries and jurisdictions globally. For example, in 2017, the country of Mongolia passed the Law on Deliberative Polling, which required the Parliament to convene a national Deliberative Poll in order to make any amendments to the country's constitution (Stanford Deliberative Democracy Lab, 2017a). Since the Law, the country has convened two national Deliberative Polls and as required by law, the Parliament reviewed the Deliberative Polling results and amended parts of the constitution. On a global scale, DDL, in partnership with Meta and the Behavioral Insights Team, conducted an online global Deliberative Poll called the Meta Community Forum, which included 32 countries, 19 languages, and over 6500 participants and a comparable size control group that did not deliberate, totaling 14,000 participants (Stanford Deliberative Democracy Lab, 2023). The topic of deliberation was policies toward bullying and harassment in the Metaverse. This project demonstrated how the public can provide input into the governance of new technologies, where Meta used the results as a part of their product and governance policies. As a further example, in 2024, in collaboration with the Trinity Challenge at Cambridge University, DDL conducted six national online Deliberative Polls on resistance to antibiotics and the policies toward antimicrobial resistance (Stanford Deliberative Democracy Lab, 2024). This project selected six global south countries to deliberate on critical policies for this pressing public health crisis. The results of this Deliberative Poll contributed to the Trinity Challenge's presentation at the UN General Assembly in 2024. Over the last few decades, there have been numerous Deliberative Polls with significant policy impact on the topic of climate and environment.

Deliberative Polling is often best used for topics that lack salience in the public. Even though discussions about climate and the environment are sometimes top of mind for the general public, the topic of SG, or even the term, is unheard of, let alone understood (Carlisle et al., 2020). For a topic that has little visibility among the public, the process of Deliberative Polling provides the time and resources for participants to learn and engage with their peers, so that they can discuss the trade offs and form their own considered opinions. Without dedicated time and space to do so, the general public is unlikely to engage and learn about SG, especially because of the reasons stated earlier regarding the problems of conventional public opinion.

Further, a critical component of the Deliberative Polling process are the balanced and vetted briefing materials and briefing videos (Fishkin, 2009). The briefing materials are developed by a working group and vetted by an advisory committee that consists of persons that represent positions from across the spectrum, whether from political party or range of opinions on the discussion topics. The list of advisory committee members are also listed visibility on the briefing materials so that participants are aware of who vetted and signed off on the materials. Having such balanced and vetted materials, allow participants to have a basic understanding of the background information on the discussion topics and also the pros and cons of the policy proposals being discussed. They may also be less likely to believe false information about SG, such as that chemtrails exist or SG is already being deployed (Buck et al., 2025).

2.4.3 Methodology

The method of Deliberative Polling includes six steps:

(1) **A random, representative sample** is first polled on the targeted issues.
(2) After this baseline poll, members of the sample are invited to gather at a single place (whether online or in-person) for at least one day (sometimes

a weekend, over several days over the course of a few weeks) in order to discuss the issues.

(3) Carefully balanced briefing materials are sent to the participants and are also made publicly available after the deliberations. The materials are vetted by an advisory committee for balance and accuracy. Briefing videos are also produced to assist participants in understanding the materials.

(4) The participants are randomly assigned to **small groups** (about 8–10 persons) and deliberate on the issues. They alternate between small group discussions and plenary sessions with experts and policymakers throughout deliberative events.

(5) The participants engage in a Q&A **dialogue with competing experts** based on questions they developed in their small group discussions.

(6) After the deliberations, the sample is again asked the original questions in a **confidential questionnaire**. The resulting opinion changes represent the conclusions the public would reach, if people had the opportunity to become informed and engaged by the issues. The results are released to the public and through media outlets.

In Figure 4, the image for small group deliberations is from the national 2015 Deliberative Poll in Tanzania about resource management. The image for expert plenary sessions is from the first national 2017 Deliberative Poll in North Macedonia about ascension to the EU.

In addition to in-person Deliberative Polls, the Deliberative Democracy Lab (DDL) at Stanford started convening online Deliberative Polls in the early 2000s. In those early events, the deliberations were synchronous but voice-only. In 2017, in collaboration with the Stanford Crowdsourced Democracy

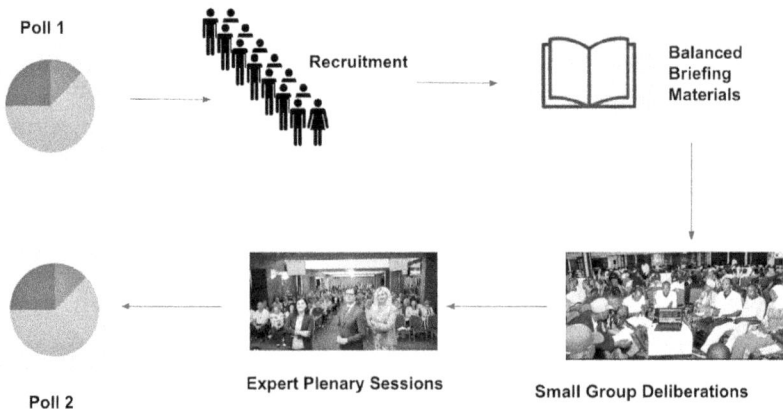

Figure 4 The Deliberative Polling process

Team, led by Ashish Goel, DDL put forth the AI-assisted Stanford Online Deliberation Platform (Figure 5). This deliberation platform features an automated moderator, which means the platform does not require a human moderator to conduct small group discussions. The platform is designed based on the decades of experience from Deliberative Polling and training of moderators. The platform features includes a speaking queue, agenda management, real-time transcriptions, and nudging of participants to join the conversations. As of fall 2024, the platform has logged over 100,000 hours of deliberation in over thirty-five countries, using more than twenty languages (Figure 6).

Though there is an effort made to standardize Deliberative Polling to ensure high-quality results, certain aspects of the model are tailored to enable success in diverse contexts. Local partners collaborate to ensure the briefing materials and survey instrument will effectively inform participants and enable meaningful deliberation. Most importantly, briefing materials and videos are designed for each Deliberative Poll to be accessible and applicable for the specific context. For example, examples are selected to be culturally appropriate and written text is tailored to match national reading levels.

2.4.4 Strengths and Limitations

Deliberative Polling represents one of several methods to engage the public in decision-making. Traditional approaches, such as town meetings and public hearings, allow for in-person gatherings where the community can come together periodically. More recently, deliberative events like citizens' assemblies have been organized by governments, civil society organizations, and nonprofits to foster structured public discussions. Additionally, asynchronous methods such as online forums and social media platforms enable broader public participation by allowing people to share their views at their convenience.

Each methodology has its strengths and limitations, serving distinct purposes in the engagement process. For instance, during the ideation phase, asynchronous platforms are highly effective for gathering a wide range of ideas and perspectives from a diverse population. This inclusivity ensures that all possible viewpoints are considered. However, after this initial stage, the results must be synthesized to focus on specific topics requiring in-depth discussion.

When deliberation is the goal, synchronous methods – such as Deliberative Polling – may be more appropriate. These approaches allow participants to engage in real-time dialogue, fostering a deeper understanding of complex issues through interaction and discussion. However, synchronous deliberation

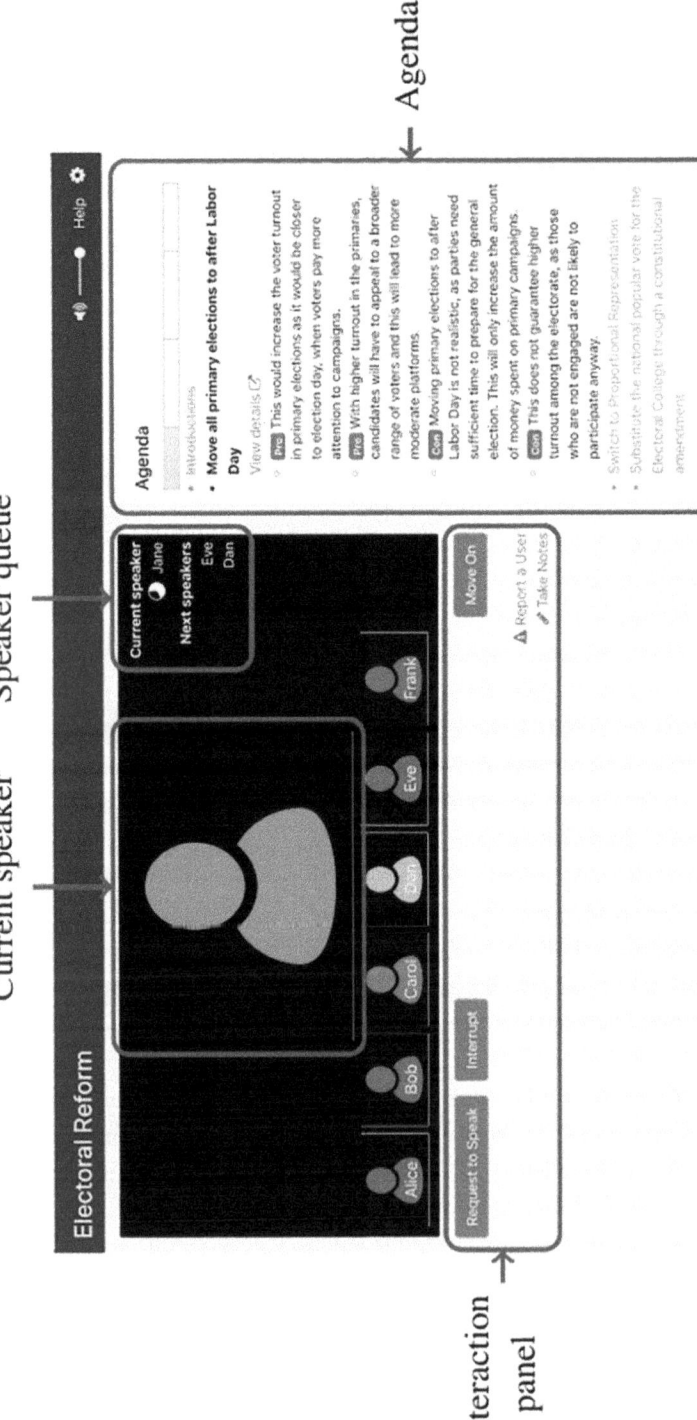

Figure 5 A snapshot of the AI-assisted Stanford Online Deliberation Platform

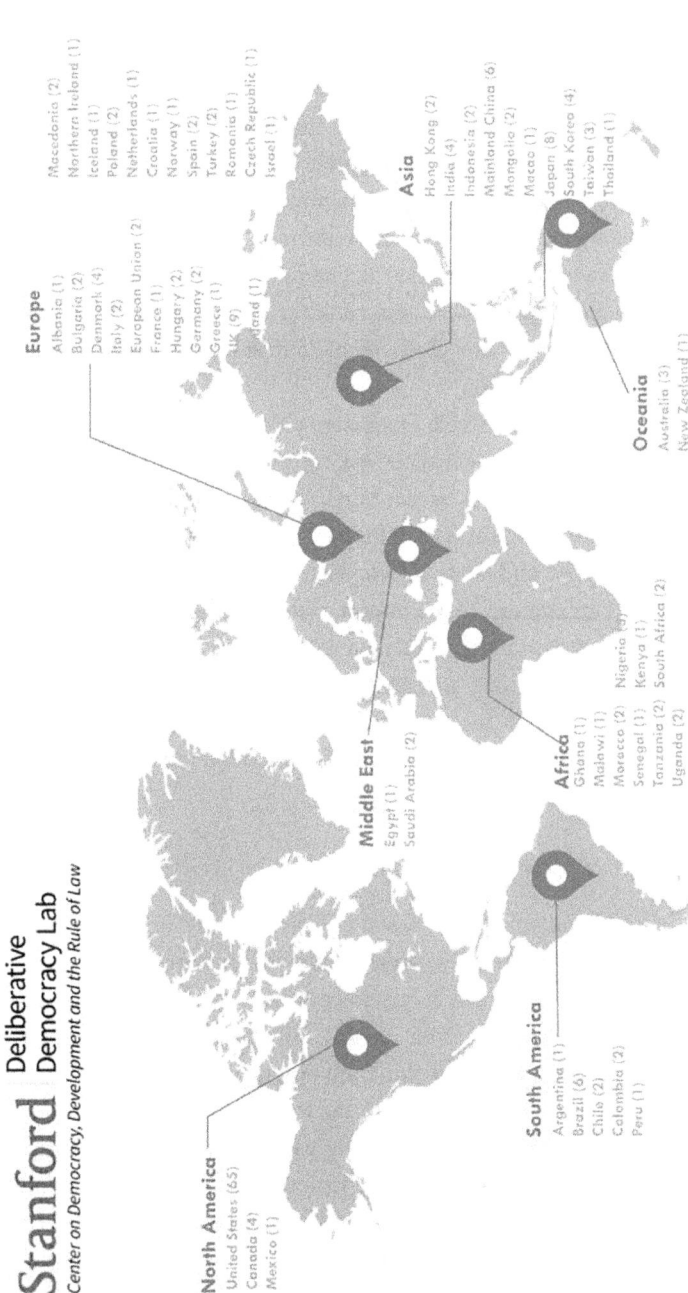

Figure 6 Map of countries where Deliberative Polling has been implemented as of November 2024.

can be time-intensive, may limit participation due to scheduling constraints, and often requires skilled facilitation to ensure constructive engagement.

Furthermore, on Deliberative Polling specifically, the time, effort, and resources required to implement a Deliberative Poll is not trivial. A 2007 European-wide Deliberative Poll sponsored by the European Commission costs over 1 million euros. This event brought together 362 participants from 27 EU countries for a 4-day deliberation together in Brussels. The majority of the costs were dedicated to the travel and accommodation costs for the participants. In contrast, using the Stanford Online Deliberation Platform, the Stanford Deliberative Democracy Lab has hosted deliberations at significantly lower costs, where a few hours of deliberations could be several thousand dollars, excluding the incentives that are given to participants as a gesture of our appreciation for their participation.

Given the time and costs involved, Deliberative Polling is valuable when it can have a tangible impact on decision-making or other courses of action, especially when interested groups or decision-makers are prepared to act on the results. If Deliberative Polling is used for purely academic purposes, that is, to understand public views and not to inform decision-making, it's important to manage participant expectations of the impact of their participation.

Though Deliberative Polling does rely on expert knowledge to design the briefing material and questions for deliberation, it can be paired with a method like pTA that builds in a process for broader participation in the framing of the issue and relevant expertise and design of questions and deliberation process.

2.4.5 Broader Implications

This method of Deliberative Polling has significant broader implications for democratic processes, policymaking, social cohesion, and governance world-wide. One of its key contributions is enhancing democratic legitimacy (Fishkin, 2009). By equipping participants with reliable information and encouraging thoughtful deliberation, the method helps form opinions based on substantive understanding rather than superficial or partisan influences. For policymakers, Deliberative Polling provides an opportunity to gauge informed public preferences, enabling decisions that better reflect societal values. It also facilitates mutual understanding by addressing polarized views in a constructive and structured manner, promoting common ground on contentious issues. Globally, Deliberative Polling has been successfully implemented across different cultural contexts, tackling issues such as climate change, education reform, and healthcare.

Beyond governance, Deliberative Polling offers significant educational benefits. Participants not only gain insights into specific issues but also develop critical thinking and communication skills that enhance their civic engagement. This learning often extends beyond the individual, as participants share their newfound understanding within their communities, influencing broader public discourse. The method challenges traditional governance by exposing the limitations of conventional representative democracy, particularly the gap between uninformed public opinion and policymaking. The methodology suggests pathways into integrating deliberative mechanisms into formal political systems to improve democratic outcomes.

As technology evolves, Deliberative Polling has leveraged digital platforms, specifically the AI-assisted Stanford Online Deliberation Platform, to engage larger populations simultaneously. The deliberation platform underscores the method's scalability and potential to address complex, multi-stakeholder challenges in an increasingly interconnected world. Overall, Deliberative Polling represents a transformative approach to decision-making, fostering a more informed and inclusive public sphere.

2.5 Conclusion

No single method can address every need for engagement on emerging technologies. The engagement methods discussed in this section have diverse aims and goals, participant audiences, facilitation requirements, and methodologies. Each method also has strengths and limitations, which may make each method more or less applicable in different contexts, depending on the purpose of the engagement, the audience, time and funding availability, and more. They also have divergent theoretical and conceptual underpinnings, and they emerged in different contexts to address a different set of problems. At the same time, all three methods also emerged in response to limitations of prior methods: DSG's capacity building workshops aim to transcend limitations of the "classic" capacity building model; participatory technology assessment was developed to fill representation gaps in traditional forms of technology assessment; and Deliberative Polling aims to overcome problems with conventional polling efforts. When used together within a broader program of engagement, these methods can complement each other by creating the conditions that enable the successful use of other methods. Their combined use can fill multiple engagement needs related to building foundational knowledge in civil society, including marginalized groups in technology assessment, and facilitating broad deliberation to inform specific decisions. Readers should consider how other methods they may be familiar with can also be combined to accomplish similar aims.

Part II Briefing Book for Engagement

3 How to Use This Briefing Book

3.1 Goals of the Briefing Book

This briefing book provides accessible, evidence-based, and balanced information on solar geoengineering (SG). It can be used to support efforts to build capacity for various types of publics to discuss this increasingly important and complex topic. The briefing book can be used to ensure participants, across a variety of engagement methods, are equipped to discuss SG's scientific, political, and ethical dimensions. Crucially, while it is essential to make information on SG available to these groups, the briefing book does not aim to tell people how or what to think about SG; this Element aims to provide engagement participants with information that may help them develop their own perspectives on SG. Coauthor Erika Check Haden is an expert in scientific communication and led our efforts to ensure we provided information that was not leading but rather balanced and accessible.

We also created a companion website that contains an extended list of public resources for further learning, including authoritative assessment reports of SG, high-level governance reports and proposals, public educational sources created by others, and other important documents for readers to continue their learning on this critical topic. All material associated with the briefing material, including the list of resources for further learning, can be found at https://www.sikinajinnah.org/geoengineering-briefing-materials.html.

To ensure the briefing book remains relevant and effective over time and across diverse contexts, we intend for the briefing book to be a collaborative living project. Specifically, we hope the materials will evolve through two processes. First, we will periodically revise the briefing materials in response to submitted feedback from users and participants and evolving scientific and governance developments in the field. Second, we encourage others to adapt the most current version of the briefing book to meet the needs of diverse audiences across different contexts. The briefing book is a model that can be adapted to meet the specific accessibility needs of particular audiences, rather than a one-size-fits-all solution, wherein one set of materials is intended to meet the unique learning needs of many different groups of people. To that end, the briefing book is fully open access and aims to be accessible to an audience of English-speaking laypersons. We encourage NGO practitioners, public engagement professionals, academics, journalists, and others involved in SG public engagement efforts to adapt this briefing book as needed to fit the accessibility and information needs of diverse audiences, such as youth, students, local communities, national or global publics, and more.

We suggest this dual adaptive process as a model that others can use to create briefing materials that can build capacity for public engagement across other issues related to emerging technologies, scientific issues, or environmental challenges. We explain our vision for each process in more detail next after first describing our process for developing the briefing book.

3.2 Briefing Book Development Process

The briefing book was developed through an iterative two year process.

First, coauthor Sikina Jinnah funded and cohosted, with coauthor Shuchi Talati (DSG), an invited workshop with the Deliberative Democracy Lab at Stanford University in May 2023 to explore issues related to SG and justice within the context of a research project aiming to explore global perspectives on SG. The workshop was attended by most of the coauthors of this Element, in addition to several other experts in SG and related fields and several undergraduate and graduate students. One of the goals of the workshop was to develop science communication skills and to create a framework for the development of a set of informational materials that could be used to inform public participants in a global perspectives research study. Participants of the workshop collaboratively developed a set of "buckets" outlining the areas of knowledge that would help enable informed participation in SG discussions. These buckets formed the basis for the sections of the briefing book.

Following the workshop, this Element's coauthors collaboratively outlined in greater detail the content that would be included in each section of the briefing book. Coauthor Zachary Dove then worked with an undergraduate student researcher to create drafts of the briefing book sections, which were iteratively reviewed by the briefing book coauthors and subsequently revised. Multiple rounds of internal revision were completed before sections of the briefing book were sent to several SG experts, including some who were in attendance at the Stanford Workshop for peer review, and then subsequently revised in line with reviewer feedback. Some sections, such as the SG science section, underwent multiple rounds of peer review with several reviewers.

Subsequent to peer review, coauthor and science communication expert Erika Check Hayden deployed evidence-based techniques to "translate" the material to be accessible for English-speaking laypersons. These techniques aim to adapt the material so that it can be understood at the average reading level for adults, and incorporate methods such as using shorter, simpler sentences and paragraphs, selecting active verbs, and eschewing or defining technical language and acronyms. All authors worked collaboratively in a final round of revision to ensure the final briefing book met standards of accuracy, balance, and accessibility.

3.3 Updating the Briefing Book

The first process we are implementing to ensure the briefing book remains relevant and effective is to update the briefing materials over time in response to submitted feedback and new developments in the field. The research and governance landscape of SG is rapidly evolving. Research publications are increasing, new research programs are on the horizon, and subnational and national governments and intergovernmental organizations are increasingly engaging in SG discussion, negotiation, and policymaking. The briefing book reflects the current state of knowledge on SG and its current governance landscape as of 2025; both of which will change as new knowledge and governance activity develop. We therefore envision updating and revising the briefing book periodically as needed to capture an evolving research and governance landscape. We also encourage feedback or suggestions for additions or revisions from a community of users, including researchers, practitioners, and others that are knowledgeable of current developments in the climate or SG field or who have used the briefing material in engagement activities.[7] Updates and revisions to the briefing materials and forms for feedback from users and participants can be found at www.sikinajinnah.org/geoengineering-briefing-materials.html.

3.4 Adapting the Briefing Book

We also invite scholars and practitioners to use and adapt the current version of the briefing book to ensure the material is relevant for different audiences. Adapting this briefing book to meet specific audiences' needs may entail translation, editing, reformatting, adding or removing content, or even changing the medium. For example, information from these briefing materials can be pulled to create media content fit for consumption on social media, where many people, including younger generations, now obtain most of their information and news (Gottfried, 2024). We discuss possibilities for adapting material for the briefing book for youth audiences in further detail next.

Additionally, the briefing materials may be more effective in certain contexts when integrated with other forms of relevant knowledge and information on

---

[7] Other topics may be included in future expanded versions of the briefing materials, such as related to the history and politics of both climate science and solar geoengineering.

issues related to climate, environment, and technology. For example, some communities may want to understand the issues and challenges related to climate change and SG through the lens of Traditional Ecological Knowledge (TEK), other forms of Indigenous knowledge as well as place-based lay knowledge (e.g., Busch et al., 2025). We take the relevance and validity of these forms of knowledge seriously. An inclusive and robust assessment and deliberation process for SG would facilitate interaction and learning across different ways of knowing. Currently the knowledge in the briefing book does come from existing expert research and discussion, which has been largely conducted in the Global North, and as such it is not intended to be exhaustive, nor to provide the authoritative and final say on these issues. Future iterations of the briefing book, as a living and collaborative document, can and should incorporate lay knowledge, Indigenous knowledge, and TEK. We also encourage the development of briefing materials designed to provide focused explorations of SG from these perspectives.

The possibility of adapting the briefing book material to fit audience needs can enable practitioners to effectively reach diverse audiences. At the same time, adapting the material raises the challenge of ensuring that the accuracy of the information is not lost through adaptation. The briefing book was designed to accurately present and characterize areas of scientific knowledge and uncertainty on an issue with a limited but evolving knowledge base. Additionally, the topic is controversial, and many of the social, political, and ethical issues that are explored have split experts. We have tried to cover these debates and disagreements through a fair and balanced presentation of the different positions and arguments that characterize much of the expert discussion on SG. We encourage those wishing to adapt the material to approach this in a similar way. To that end, those adapting the briefing book should endeavor to conduct a peer review of any adapted material, and follow other relevant procedures to ensure the information is valid. Integrating lay knowledge into these materials should not include misinformation or falsehoods about SG and chemtrails, for example.

We suggest that those wishing to use our briefing materials should first test the effectiveness and relevancy of the material through a "pilot" engagement prior to initiating engagement activities. The pilot engagement could be used to test how well the briefing materials enable informed discussion within a sample from a specific audience, and it can help researchers or practitioners learn what information, issues, questions, or knowledge is missing, how certain framings of SG shape discussion, and how the materials need to be adapted to be most effective for use in specific contexts.

3.5 Translating for Youth Audience

Project collaborators hope that the briefing book can be used to inform, educate, and engage youth audiences. Best practices for reaching youth audiences should include developing campaigns to reach youth in specific cultural settings. Different parts of these materials will likely resonate with youth of different ages, geographic locations, and sociocultural contexts. Local partners who work with youth will be best positioned to decide which parts of these materials will be most relevant and relatable to their youth audiences, and to adapt them to the needs and interests of the youth populations that they serve.

Reaching youth will require communicating with youth where they are, whether that comes in the form of in-person activities in schools, after-school activities or community centers, or through social media, which is one of the main vehicles that youth use to communicate. It's also critical to adapt any communication campaign based on the learnings gleaned from these campaigns, as there have been few direct outreach efforts focused on measuring youth engagement with the science, justice, ethics, and governance issues related to geoengineering.

4 Climate Science

4.1 Introduction

Has the weather where you lived changed recently? Your seasons may feel different. Your summers may be hotter and your winters may be colder. Or you might have less snow in the winter. You may also have had droughts, wildfires, or storms.

Some of these things are happening because the Earth's global weather patterns are changing through a process called **climate change**. The planet's climate, or overall average weather conditions, is not the same as it was 100 years ago. Earth's surface is warming. And rainfall patterns are changing. Severe and extreme weather have hit many communities hard.

Human activities are causing this global climate change. By driving cars, farming, and producing electricity, we release chemicals called **greenhouse gasses** into the air. (Watch this video https://www.youtube.com/watch?v=wzPUm-Ytpz4 from NASA on how we know the climate is changing.) Released greenhouse gasses are called greenhouse gas **emissions**.

The world's climate experts agree that people are causing climate change, and if steps are not taken immediately, the world will face severe impacts. These experts meet in a group called **The Intergovernmental Panel on Climate Change** (IPCC).

This section explains how greenhouse gasses are causing climate change and how that could impact our world.

4.2 How Does the Climate Work?

Two main factors control the Earth's climate: the amount of incoming sunlight that is absorbed or reflected, and the heat trapping effect of various gasses in the Earth's atmosphere, which is the layer of gasses that surrounds the Earth and separates its surface from space. Sunlight absorbed in the atmosphere or at the surface is converted into heat. That heat eventually escapes into space. But certain gasses, called greenhouse gasses, trap the heat as it passes through the atmosphere. The most common of these greenhouse gasses are called carbon dioxide and methane, but others are important too. They are called greenhouse gasses because they act like the glass in a gardener's greenhouse, trapping heat before it can escape.

4.3 Where Does Climate Change Come From?

The amount of carbon dioxide in the Earth's atmosphere has varied with the same range for the past 2.5 million years. However, starting with the Industrial Revolution in the 1800s, the amount of carbon dioxide in the atmosphere began to increase above these levels. Carbon dioxide is a greenhouse gas, so the Earth's climate began to warm as more heat was trapped. In 2011–2020, the global surface temperature increased 1.1°C (2°F) since the last half of the nineteenth century.[8] In 2024, the warmest year on record, global temperatures rose 1.5°C above preindustrial levels, approaching a threshold that global leaders have pledged to avoid.[9]

What changed? Starting in the 1800s, inventors created new ways to use energy to make our lives easier. For instance, they made light bulbs and car engines. They began making fertilizer in factories to help crops grow.

These inventions need energy to work. To make this energy, people burned materials including coal, oil, and natural gas. These materials are called **fossil fuels**, because they come from the breakdown of ancient life forms underground in the form of fossils. Most of our energy still comes from fossil fuels today.

When we burn fossil fuels, we release energy to power everyday things like refrigerators and mobile phone batteries. Fossil fuels also power many of our cars, ships, trains, and planes that we use to transport products and travel, and it powers the manufacturing and industrial operations that provide us with products we use. However, burning fossil fuels also releases greenhouse gasses into the air.

---

[8] Calvin et al. (2023) [9] United Nations (2025)

Other human activities also contribute to climate change. For example, we raise large numbers of cattle for dairy and meat. However, cattle release methane as they digest food.[10] Also, when we cut down trees, such as to create more land for growing food, we release the carbon dioxide the trees stored as they grew.

Greenhouse gasses are also released through natural processes. However, experts agree the large amounts of greenhouse gasses released by humans are mainly responsible for causing climate change.[11]

Not all humans contribute the same amount to climate change – some countries have released much more carbon dioxide than others, and within countries, some wealthier people emit much more carbon dioxide than poor people.

4.4 Why Are Greenhouse Gasses Important?

When the sun shines down through the glass walls and ceiling of a greenhouse, the glass traps heat from the sun's rays inside the greenhouse. So it's warmer inside the greenhouse than outside.

Similarly, greenhouse gasses such as carbon dioxide and methane trap heat in the Earth's atmosphere As greenhouse gasses trap heat in the atmosphere, this creates what scientists call the **greenhouse effect**. (Watch this video https://www.youtube.com/watch?v=SN5-DnOHQmE from NASA on the greenhouse effect.) Greenhouse gasses act as a blanket around the Earth, trapping heat that would normally escape into space. This raises Earth's average temperature. This causes climate change. As more greenhouse gasses are released into the atmosphere, more heat is trapped in the atmosphere, and the more the climate changes. Figure 7 shows how the Earth's rising surface temperature is directly linked to increasing amounts of carbon dioxide in the atmosphere. Red and blue bars indicate differences in temperatures for each year from long-term averages. Red bars show temperatures above the long-term average and blue lines indicate temperatures below the long-term average. The gray line charts the amount of carbon dioxide in the atmosphere in parts per million (ppm). Scientists are confident that temperatures will continue to rise for many decades.

4.5 How Is the Climate Changing?

As more heat is trapped in the atmosphere, weather patterns become more extreme and change in different ways, including in precipitation (such as prolonged drought and heavy rain seasons) and rising surface temperatures. Climate change affects every place differently. Temperature and rainfall will change more in some areas than in others. (Watch this video

---

[10] Grossi et al. (2019)   [11] Calvin et al. (2023)

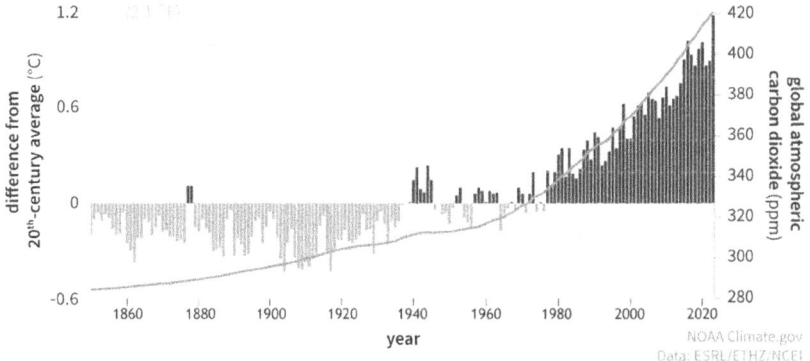

Figure 7 Rising surface temperatures are directly linked to the amount of carbon dioxide in the atmosphere.

Source: NOAA climate.gov

https://www.youtube.com/watch?v=G4H1N_yXBiA from National Geographic on the causes and impacts of climate change.) Here are some examples of climate change impacts around the world:

Extreme heat has become more common almost everywhere. Extreme heat means a series of days with very high temperatures and humidity – for instance, more than two to three days of temperatures above 32°C. Extreme heat is deadly. In 2022, for example, extreme heat killed more than 60,000 people in Europe.[12] (Watch this NASA video https://www.youtube.com/watch?v=8ZdDWQTgP2Y on record high temperatures in summer 2023.)

Heavy rainfall has caused flooding around the world, especially in Europe and Asia. For instance, flooding caused the deaths of 152,753 infants in Bangladesh from 1988 to 2017, one study estimated.[13] Scientists predict that flooding will be the leading cause[14] of deaths linked to climate change by 2050.

Higher temperatures are causing more serious, longer **droughts** in Africa, southern Europe, and North and South America. Droughts happen when there isn't enough rain for a long time. They kill crops and dry up water sources that people and animals need to survive. For instance, droughts killed[15] 43,000 people in Somalia in 2022, more than half of them children. Droughts also contribute to disasters such as wildfires.

As the climate warms, drier regions can typically anticipate overall less rain leading to increased drought, and regions with more rainfall can typically anticipate even more rain leading to increases of flooding and related issues.

---

[12] Ballester et al. (2023)   [13] Rerolle et al. (2023)   [14] Eitelwein et al. (2024)
[15] WHO and UNICEF (2023)

Extreme weather events like droughts, hurricanes, cold fronts, and heat waves won't behave like they have in the past. They might happen more often or be stronger. When these kinds of weather events get worse, they can hurt people and damage the environment.

Additionally, oceans absorb carbon dioxide. As we release more carbon dioxide into the atmosphere, the oceans absorb more, causing **oceans to become more acidic,** killing sea life such as coral reefs.

Sea level rise also occurs as sea ice and glaciers melt and add water to the ocean, and as ocean water expands due to warmer ocean temperatures. As the sea level rises, more land along the coast is swallowed by the ocean. This causes flooding, erosion of the land, and more danger from storms. Entire areas and even some low-lying islands will become entirely uninhabitable.

Overall, climate change will have widespread and damaging impacts across the world. However, the impacts will depend on how much greenhouse gasses we continue to release into the atmosphere. While some impacts are now unavoidable, we may be able to avoid some of the worst impacts by reducing our emissions.

4.6 How Does Climate Change Affect Plants and Animals?

Climate change will damage **biodiversity**. Biodiversity means the variety of different plants, animals, and bugs living in different places, and also the food chain that connects these living organisms. As the Earth and oceans get warmer, many living things are feeling the effects already.

Many living things only survive in certain conditions, such as specific temperatures and humidity levels. They live in places that have just the right environment for them. But climate change is disrupting this balance. Now, some living things can't survive in the places where they have thrived for thousands of years due to changes in temperature or precipitation in the area. Some species are trying to move to find better homes, but not all of them can. This means many species are going extinct, disappearing forever because of climate change.

Coral reefs are a good example of this. Ocean water is getting hotter and more acidic. This has caused coral bleaching, when coral turns white and dies. It's happening in many places around the world, most notably in the Great Barrier Reef off the coast of Australia. Lots of coral species might disappear completely, which also harms the many species that use coral as habitat.

4.7 How Does Climate Change Affect People's Health?

Climate change affects people's health and how they feel. For instance, when extreme weather like heatwaves, storms, and wildfires happen more often and become more intense, they hurt people and can even cause many deaths.[16] Higher outdoor temperatures are already causing more people to die from hot weather.[17] These kinds of disasters can also make it harder to get food and water, because the weather changes how well crops grow and can lead to droughts, when people can't get enough water. Access to food and water is vital for good health. Parasites and pathogens are also expected to travel to new areas as habitats break down, exposing more humans to dangerous disease.

Climate change doesn't just affect our bodies; it can also make us feel stressed and worried about the future. This can lead to something called climate anxiety, where people feel really anxious because of climate change.[18] Younger people might feel this more because they know they'll have to deal with the effects of climate change for longer.

The heat that comes with climate change can also make people more cranky and aggressive, which isn't good for anyone's mental health. So, climate change isn't just about the weather – it's also about how it makes us feel and how it affects our health.

4.8 How Does Climate Change Affect Human Society?

Climate change disrupts important systems that keep our world running. For instance, the power could go out because people are using more heat or air conditioning than usual. Intense storms could knock out water pumps that prevent flooding. Extreme weather could damage roads, railroads, ports, and transportation hubs. Damage to infrastructure including transportation, water, sanitation, and energy leads to economic losses, disruptions of essential services, and harmful impacts on well-being.

Anything that is near the coast – roads, factories, farms, and houses – is at risk of being damaged due to sea level rise. Billions of people live near the coast, and eight of the ten largest cities in the world are built along the coast.[19] The sea level has risen on average 8–9 inches since 1880 and will continue to rise depending on how much climate change worsens.

Climate change can also cause human conflict and suffering. For instance, people must flee their homes to get away from problems, including drought and sea level rise. People in other countries may not want to help these climate refugees. People may also fight over increasingly scarce resources.

Climate change is also expected to create large economic losses and damages including in certain sectors such as agriculture. This will impact people's livelihoods and their ability to meet their basic needs.

---

[16] Loucks (2021)   [17] Vicedo-Cabrera et al. (2021)   [18] Clayton (2020)
[19] UN Atlas of the Ocean. n.d.

Climate change may also have harmful impacts on human culture as people face loss of ecosystems or are forced to migrate away from ancestral territories. This is particularly true for Indigenous peoples and local communities who depend on ecosystems to meet basic needs.

4.8.1 Climate Change Could Worsen Inequality

Climate change doesn't impact everyone the same way. The harmful impacts discussed earlier are generally concentrated among people who are poorer and have historically and currently faced discrimination because of their gender, race, ethnicity, or for other reasons. These groups are most vulnerable to climate change, which means that they are most at risk of being harmed by it. For instance, some people can't afford to pay for air conditioning to cool their homes during heat waves. Others may not be able to move to safer locations, or they may be more likely to lose access to shelter, food, and water.

4.9 How Do We Know What We Know about Climate Change?

A lot of what we know about the future impacts of climate change comes from something called **climate models**. These aren't the same kinds of toy models that you might buy and build, like model airplanes or cars. Instead, these models are complex computer programs that scientists use to understand how climate change works. We also know a lot about historical changes in the climate by studying the natural world, such as by looking at ice in Antarctica, and also from our understanding of basic physics, such as the laws of thermodynamics.

Scientists use climate models to predict what might happen because of climate change and what might happen if people do   or don't do – different things to stop it. This helps us see how we've changed the climate already and how the climate could continue to change in the future. (Watch this PBS video https://www.youtube.com/watch?v=dGF4-JyHh_8 on climate models.)

But these models aren't perfect. They can't include every detail of how the Earth's climate works, so it's hard to make exact predictions about what will happen and when.

Scientists have used climate models and other models called integrated assessment models to show that the world is on track to warm well above levels that are considered manageable. In 2015, 196 countries set a target in what is called the United Nations' Paris Agreement on climate change. They agreed to work together to prevent dangerous climate changes by taking action to limit warming to well below 2°C (3.8°F) above preindustrial levels. Even this rise in temperature will still cause a huge amount of damage. (Watch this PBS video: https://www.youtube.com/watch?v=6cRCbgTA_78 "What's the Big Deal with a Few Degrees?")

But scientists have shown that we're not doing nearly enough to meet that goal. As temperatures rise, the costs and consequences of climate change become worse. If we want to have a reasonable chance of preventing some of the worst impacts of climate change, we're going to need to do much more.

5 Climate Policy

5.1 Introduction

There are different ways of tackling climate change, **called climate action**. Scientists and policymakers have until recently mostly discussed two main forms of climate action: mitigation and adaptation.

We can **mitigate**, or lessen, climate change by cutting greenhouse gas emissions. We can also **adapt** to climate change by making changes to our infrastructure, economy, agriculture, cities, or countries to better handle the impacts of climate change. While mitigation aims at preventing climate change from occurring or worsening, adaptation aims to improve our ability to cope with climate impacts that arise from previous emissions. **Climate policy** refers to laws, rules, and legislation that address climate change, for example by requiring or encouraging various forms of mitigation or adaptation.

Recently, scientists and policymakers embraced a third form of climate action. Carbon dioxide removal (CDR), also called negative emission technologies (NETs), would aim to remove previously released carbon dioxide from the atmosphere. Scientists are also exploring a potential fourth form of climate action, called solar geoengineering.[20] This method would involve deflecting sunlight away from the planet to lower the planet's temperature thereby reducing some climate impacts (Section 6).

Today, climate policy is increasingly important. Many countries, local governments, businesses, and other organizations are becoming involved in planning and taking climate action. Many people agree that we need to work hard to stop releasing so much climate change causing greenhouse gasses and help people adapt to climate change. This section explains how people are working right now to prevent and respond to climate change.

5.2 Mitigation: Reducing Greenhouse Gas Emissions

Mitigation means cutting greenhouse gas emissions. This reduces the harmful effects of climate change by preventing more carbon dioxide from being released into the atmosphere.

---

[20] MacMartin et al. (2018)

Mitigation actions can come in different forms. They can include policies to promote reductions in greenhouse gas emissions by offering tax benefits for people, businesses, and governments to shift away from fossil fuels. They can also include supporting cleaner technology and infrastructure, such as investing in building more solar power plants, which do not contribute to climate change. Electrifying transportation options and decreasing how much energy products or vehicles use can also cut emissions. And mitigation can also mean changing the way people use land, such as slowing or preventing the destruction of forests.

Governments sometimes require these steps. But businesses and individuals can also take part voluntarily. For instance, businesses can choose to reduce the amount of energy they use to produce their products. And people can choose to buy a compact car rather than a large truck, or they can buy an electric or hybrid vehicle instead of one that runs on gasoline. Most climate policies are designed to encourage businesses and individuals to take mitigation action on their own, often through providing tax benefits and other incentives, subsidies, or information.

5.3 Adaptation: Helping People Live with Climate Change

Adaptation involves making changes to infrastructure, economies, agriculture, and other areas of society to improve how we deal with the impacts from climate change.

The climate is already changing, and many people are already experiencing harmful impacts from climate change. And we continue to release more climate change-causing gasses into the air every day, meaning climate impacts will continue to get worse. So it's becoming increasingly important to help people cope with the impacts of climate change that are already happening, and will continue to get worse.[21]

Adaptation can take many forms, including building seawalls to address sea level rise, restoring wetlands to lessen storm damage to coastlines, changing what crops we grow and how we grow them to produce more food, and creating green spaces in cities to manage heat.[22]

Humans have a long history of adapting to our environment. At the same time, there are limits to adaptation. Some experts worry that climate change may be so severe or may happen so quickly that adaptation to some impacts may no longer be possible.

---

[21] Calvin et al. (2023)   [22] Calvin et al. (2023)

5.4 Global Action: Countries Work Together to Fight Climate Change

Climate action occurs at different levels around the world, including by individuals, local communities, state or provincial governments, national governments, and all the way to international organizations such as the United Nations. Some forms of climate action, such as adaptation, mostly happen at a local level.

At the same time, climate change is a global issue. Everyone in the world, in every nation, is affected by climate change. And no country or person can solve this problem alone.

This means that countries must work together to combat climate change. To do so, countries create international climate policy, which are agreements or treaties that are negotiated between countries. These international legal agreements are supposed to guide how countries cooperate to fight climate change.

The **United Nations Framework Convention on Climate Change (UNFCCC)**, which involves all United Nations member countries, is an important agreement that aims to avoid dangerous impacts of climate change by limiting the amount of greenhouse gasses that countries release into the atmosphere.

The UNFCCC created a process for countries to determine how they will achieve this goal. The members of the agreement meet each year to discuss progress and sometimes negotiate new agreements. The UNFCCC also established that countries have "common but differentiated responsibilities," which means that although all states have some responsibility to address climate change, richer countries have more responsibility, because they have historically released far more greenhouse gasses into the atmosphere. Richer countries then should be first to reduce their emissions and they should also provide funding, technology, knowledge, and other forms of assistance to poorer countries.

At the annual meeting in Paris in 2015, countries negotiated a major agreement called the **Paris Agreement.** They agreed to keep global temperature increases to well below 2°C above preindustrial levels, and ideally to keep the increase to 1.5°C above preindustrial levels. (Preindustrial means the time before humans started releasing greenhouse gasses into the atmosphere.)

Previous treaties negotiated within the UNFCCC, such as the Kyoto Protocol, set requirements for how much each country needed to reduce their greenhouse gas emissions. Richer countries were required to reduce their emissions sooner and more drastically. However, under the Paris Agreement, each country must submit their own plan, or pledge, for how they will contribute to achieving the temperature goals. While this allows countries the flexibility to decide what climate actions are best for their own circumstances, these plans don't go far enough. Even if every country takes every step outlined in its plans, the world is still not doing nearly enough to keep climate change below 1.5°C.

In fact, the world is now on track to warm by almost 3°C and possibly more by the end of this century.[23] That's a lot more than the 1.5 degree Celsius goal set by the Paris Agreement. And it will expose the planet to dangerous and severe impacts.[24] This means that countries must make and carry out plans that are far more ambitious than they are currently to have a reasonable chance of meeting our temperature targets.

5.5 Translating International Commitments into Action

After countries agreed to limit warming in international agreements, each country must then take action within their own country. How will this happen?

National policies that address climate change manage how people, businesses, cities, and other important entities carry out actions to mitigate or adapt to climate change. Many examples of national climate policies are discussed earlier in the sections on mitigation and adaptation.

In the past decade, various regions, cities, community groups, businesses, and nongovernmental organizations have also taken steps to promote climate action.[25] They have done so even when they are not required to. Efforts such as certifying and labeling products that do not release greenhouse gasses, creating rules that businesses adopt to reduce their emissions, sharing policies, and reporting emissions reductions all contribute to climate action.[26]

5.6 Portfolios of Climate Responses

There are many different ways to address climate change. The steps countries take to manage climate action often look different. The combination of ways that each country uses to address climate change are called **portfolios of climate responses**. Every country's climate response portfolio is unique, depending on each country's interests and ability to devote time, resources, money, and energy to different mixes of policies and responses.

It's important to remember this when we think about new forms of climate action. For instance, earlier in this section, we discussed the idea of solar geoengineering, which aims to cool the planet by reflecting sunlight. One important thing to think about when considering solar geoengineering is how it will fit together with mitigation (cutting emissions of greenhouse gasses), adaptation (learning how to better deal with climate impacts), and carbon

---

[23] Calvin et al. (2023).   [24] Calvin et al. (2023).   [25] Hale et al. (2021).
[26] Gordon and Johnson (2018)

dioxide removal (removing carbon dioxide from the atmosphere). Carbon dioxide removal includes strategies that enhance the ability of agricultural land, soils, wetlands, marshes, mangroves, and forests to absorb carbon dioxide from the air and store it in biomass or organic material, and it also includes technology-based strategies. Examples of technology-based carbon dioxide removal strategies include **bioenergy with carbon capture and sequestration** (BECCS) which removes carbon dioxide in the atmosphere by burning plants that capture carbon dioxide to grow, capturing the released carbon dioxide, and then storing it underground where it cannot contribute to climate change. **Direct air capture and sequestration** (DACS) would use chemical reactions to filter carbon dioxide out of the atmosphere and then store the carbon dioxide underground.

While some believe that solar geoengineering could complement these other forms of climate action (Section 6), others are worried that paying attention to solar geoengineering will mean less mitigation action will take place (Section 7).

Solar geoengineering might be a useful tool that helps the world achieve its temperature targets, but it has its own risks.[27] Research on solar geoengineering is at an early stage, and there is still a lot we don't know.

6 Solar Geoengineering Science

6.1 Introduction

Some scientists, policymakers, and others interested in how to respond to climate change have proposed to use a method called **solar geoengineering** to address climate change. The term "solar geoengineering" includes a variety of possible ways to cool the planet down by reflecting sunlight away from Earth. Greenhouse gasses released by humans reduce the amount of energy radiated to space, causing warming (Section 4). The idea behind solar geoengineering is to lessen some of the impacts of warming caused by greenhouse gasses by reflecting sunlight (and therefore heat) away from the Earth. Because the world is on track to warm beyond internationally agreed temperature goals (Section 5), some scientists suggest that we should study different methods of solar geoengineering to better understand how it might work.

This section describes what we know and don't know about the science of solar geoengineering, and how some scientists propose to study it. Solar geoengineering is a new technology, and we don't fully understand yet how it could reduce climate change, or how it might also affect the planet and the plants,

---

[27] MacMartin et al. (2018)

animals, and people that live here.[28] Further research could help us answer these questions and inform decisions about whether and how to use solar geoengineering. Scientists working on this issue generally agree that we need to understand this technology more before we consider whether to use it or not.

6.2 Proposed Solar Geoengineering Methods

While there are many different ideas for solar geoengineering technologies, this section focuses on two methods: stratospheric aerosol injection (SAI) and marine cloud brightening (MCB). The idea behind both of these concepts is that they could reflect enough sunlight to cool the Earth. But each method has its own possible risks and benefits, as we explain next. See Figure 8 for an illustration of these methods.

6.2.1 Stratospheric Aerosol Injection

Stratospheric aerosol injection (SAI) is a proposed method for cooling the planet by placing small particles, or **aerosols**, in the air far above Earth. This would involve releasing these small particles into a layer of the planet's atmosphere called the **stratosphere**, which extends from about 10–50 kilometers above the ground at different areas around the world. (For reference, the San Francisco Bay Bridge is just under 10 kilometers long (7.18 kilometers), while San Francisco is just about 50 kilometers from Palo Alto (53 kilometers).) The aerosols would reflect a small amount of incoming sunlight back into space. That's why this technology is called stratospheric aerosol injection because it involves **injecting** small particles (**aerosols**) very high in the sky (into the **stratosphere**). The idea behind this technique is that each small particle injected into the sky would act like a tiny mirror that reflects incoming sunlight back into space. Balloons or airplanes could deliver the particles high into the sky, where the particles would remain for 1–2 years before falling back to the ground in raindrops.

Why do scientists think that injecting small particles high in the sky could cool the Earth? Because we already know that this happens after very large volcanic eruptions. These large eruptions release sulfur dioxide (SO_2) into the stratosphere, where it forms into sulfate particles that reflect sunlight away from Earth, and cool the planet. For example, scientists estimate that the 1991 eruption of Mt. Pinatubo in the Philippines lowered global average temperatures by about 0.5°C for at least a year.[29]

---

[28] National Academies of Sciences, Engineering, and Medicine (2021). This section relies extensively on NASEM 2021 for factual information about SG and its research. Other sources are cited where used.

[29] IPCC (2014)

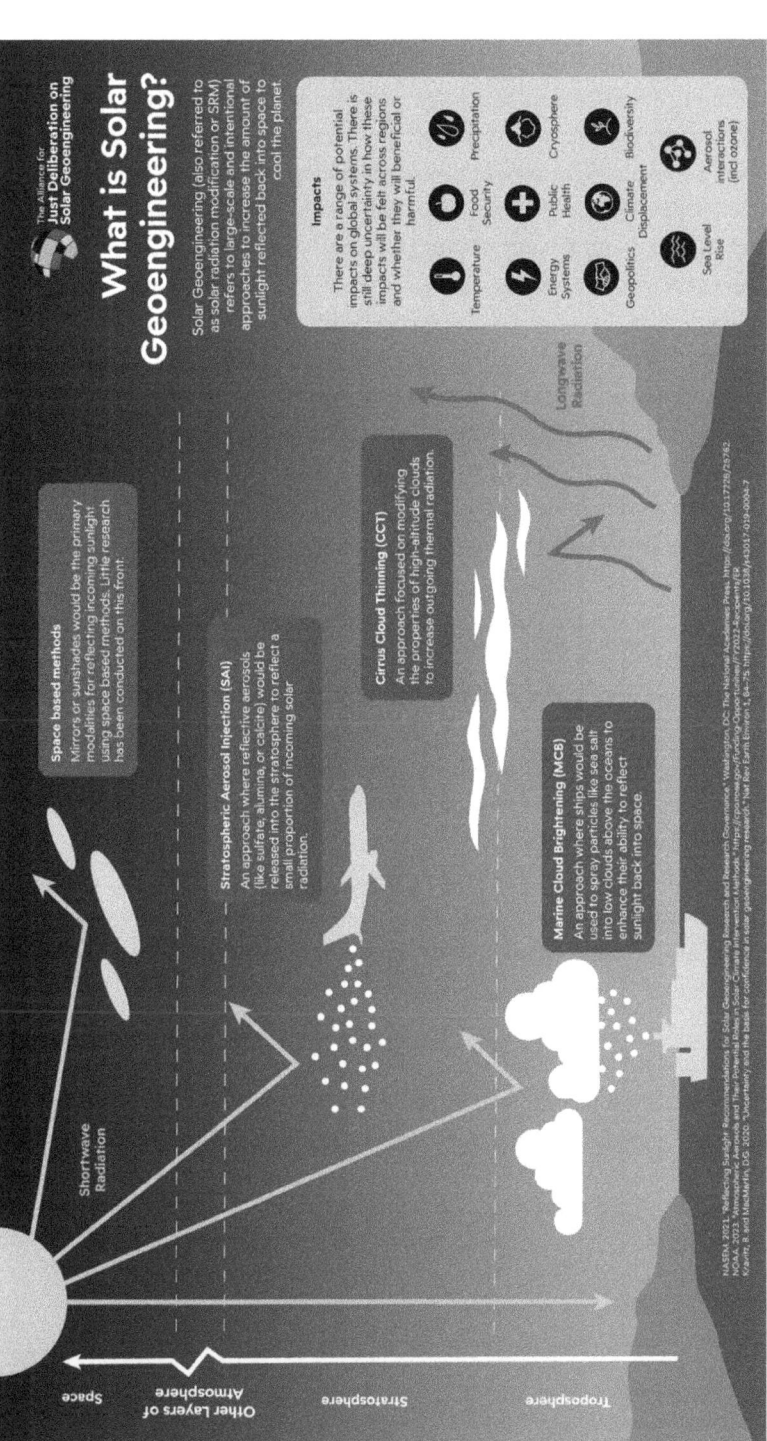

Figure 8 Illustration of proposed solar geoengineering methods. A larger version of this figure is available to view online at www.cambridge .org/jimah-et-al

Source: The Alliance for Just Deliberation on Solar Geoengineering.

Scientists say that stratospheric aerosol injection could be used to produce this cooling effect on purpose by placing sulfur or other particles high above Earth, where strong winds would blow the particles around, spreading the cooling effect far from the area where the particles were injected.

The effects of stratospheric aerosol injection would depend on how it is used, including which aerosol particles are used, how much is used, and where and when they are delivered into the sky. Different choices would create different temperature and precipitation changes in different regions of the world. For example, some scientists have explored the possibility that injecting aerosols closer to the Arctic would create greater cooling in the Arctic than elsewhere, which would slow ice loss in the Arctic and limit sea level rise.[30]

Researchers have estimated that this technology could cost several billion US dollars to upward of US$15 billion per year.[31] For instance, it would cost more to use the technology to achieve more cooling. But we would also likely need to spend several billion US dollars to build the technology.[32] This is because our existing aircraft could only release aerosol particles at about 13 kilometers above the surface, so we would need to develop new aircraft that can fly higher. Only a handful of countries have the time, money, and mature aerospace industry required to do this.[33] The full costs of a solar geoengineering deployment may be much higher when accounting for other costs, such as compensating people who are harmed by a deployment's side effects.

Scientists are studying using sulfates as a reflective material because we know more about how these particles would affect the climate, thanks to observations of sulfates and their effects following volcanic eruptions. However, sulfates also have other side effects; they would lead to a small increase in acid rain in some regions, and they could have an effect on the ozone layer that shields Earth's surface from harmful ultraviolet radiation.[34] As a result, some scientists are also considering the use of other particles, such as calcite. However, scientists don't know how these particles would interact with other gasses and material in the stratosphere, and they cannot use natural processes, such as volcanoes, to learn more about these particles' effects.

6.2.2 Marine Cloud Brightening

The other solar geoengineering method we will discuss here is marine cloud brightening (MCB). This is a proposed strategy for cooling the planet by increasing the amount of sunlight reflected by low-lying clouds over the

---

[30] E.g., Tilmes et al. (2014); Jackson et al. (2015)   [31] E.g., Smith and Wagner (2018).
[32] Smith and Wagner (2018); Janssens et al. (2020)   [33] Horton et al. (2025)
[34] Eastham et al. (2018)

ocean. This is one key difference between stratospheric aerosol injection and marine cloud brightening: In stratospheric aerosol injection, planes or balloons would inject small particles very high into the sky; but in marine cloud brightening, scientists aim to alter clouds that are much closer to the Earth's surface.

Clouds naturally contain small particles, or aerosols, such as dust, salt crystals, or dirt. Clouds form when water sticks to these tiny particles to form a **cloud droplet**. The number and size of these cloud droplets affects how much sunlight a cloud reflects. If two clouds contain the same amount of water, the cloud with more small droplets usually reflects more sunlight than the cloud with fewer large droplets. Smaller cloud droplets also prevent rain from forming, which may cause clouds to last longer and appear thicker.

Scientists have proposed the possibility that adding sea salt or other particles into the air just above the ocean could increase the amount of small cloud droplets, creating more reflective clouds. People may create this effect using a boat to spray sea water mist into the lower sky. This technology would in some ways mimic "ship tracks," which are narrow lines of clouds that sometimes form around the small particles present in ships' engine exhaust.

This raises another key difference between stratospheric aerosol injection and marine cloud brightening: the former could cool the entire world, while the latter could theoretically target specific regions for cooling. For example, researchers in Australia are exploring whether cloud brightening can cool the waters around the Great Barrier Reef off the coast of Australia. They hope this would reduce mass bleaching events, which are driving coral reefs to extinction.[35]

Marine cloud brightening could work only where there are already low-lying marine clouds, meaning would only work well in certain areas of the ocean. But even if it is only aimed at cooling specific regions, other areas could also be affected as the atmosphere redistributes heat. If marine cloud brightening were used to try to cool the entire planet, it would also cause temperatures and rain or snowfall to change a lot more in some regions of the world than under stratospheric aerosol injection.

Scientists know that adding aerosols to marine clouds can, under the right conditions, increase clouds' reflectivity. However, under other conditions, adding aerosols could make clouds evaporate more quickly, or could lower reflectivity nearby. We don't fully understand how aerosols and clouds interact, and it's difficult for scientists to answer these questions using large computer programs, or climate models, on their own. So if we really want to better

---

[35] Condie et al. (2021)

understand where, when, and how much marine clouds can be brightened, proponents say we must run experiments outside, in the real world.

Scientists and engineers must also create the right tools to brighten clouds. They'll need to spray large amounts of tiny particles, probably from a ship or a low-flying airplane, to create the effect. The challenge would be to create a system for spraying large amounts of small enough particles. They have tested some prototype spray nozzles in laboratories, and in small outdoor experiments in Australia[36] and the San Francisco Bay in the United States.[37] Further research and development would be needed to scale up these systems. And no one has thoroughly estimated how much it would cost to deploy marine cloud brightening.

6.3 Solar Geoengineering Cannot Solve Climate Change on Its Own

Solar geoengineering is not a substitute for mitigation, which is the act of reducing greenhouse gasses, and it cannot reverse all of the risks of climate change. It is also not a substitute for adaptation, which involves making changes to society and infrastructure to better deal with the consequences of climate change. To understand why, it's important to remember what causes climate change. Climate change is happening because humans are releasing large amounts of certain gasses into the air, via activities such as burning gasoline in our cars and raising animals to eat. These gasses – the greenhouse gasses, including carbon dioxide – trap energy from the sun's rays. This trapped energy cannot escape back into space, and it stays near Earth, heating up our land and oceans.

Solar geoengineering does not stop humans from producing greenhouse gasses, and it also does not decrease the amount of these gasses in the air. Remember, some greenhouse gasses stay in the atmosphere for hundreds of years. So as long as people keep producing greenhouse gasses, climate change will keep getting worse. If emissions don't stop, then the amount of solar geoengineering needed to overcome the warming effects of more and more carbon dioxide in the atmosphere would have to increase, taking the climate farther and farther into unknown and riskier conditions.

This also means that solar geoengineering would not eliminate all of the harmful impacts of climate change. For instance, because it does not decrease greenhouse gas levels, solar geoengineering would not lessen climate impacts that are directly related to how much greenhouse gas we have in the atmosphere. For example, the most important greenhouse gas released by humans, carbon dioxide, dissolves in the ocean and makes the ocean more acidic, a process

---

[36] Nelson (2020)   [37] Flavelle and Bates (2024)

called ocean acidification (Section 4). Together with higher temperatures, ocean acidification causes the death of coral reefs worldwide. Even if people use solar geoengineering to cool the ocean, this would not stop ocean acidification because it does not remove carbon dioxide from the ocean.

Moreover, if people ever use or test solar geoengineering on a large scale, it could also create new risks to the Earth and its climate, such as affecting the ozone layer that shields Earth from harmful ultraviolet radiation.[38] It may also cause other unintended consequences. For example, solar geoengineering would not exactly reverse regional weather shifts due to climate change. Instead, it would produce a new climate, not return us to the previous one. Additionally, if people start and then stop using the technology suddenly, it could trigger a sharp rise in temperatures, called a **termination shock**. To avoid a termination shock, people would have to keep using solar geoengineering for long periods of time, until the amount of carbon dioxide and other greenhouse gasses in the atmosphere return to safe levels.

For all these reasons, proponents of solar geoengineering research agree that solar geoengineering cannot solve climate change on its own and should never be a substitute for other climate responses. It should only be used as a temporary measure, and only if people are working at the same time to reduce the amount of greenhouse gasses emitted into the air, remove carbon dioxide from the atmosphere, and take steps to adapt to the impacts of climate change.

6.4 Why Consider Solar Geoengineering as a Climate Response Option?

If solar geoengineering cannot solve climate change on its own, why do some scientists, policymakers, and others say we should consider it as an option? Let's start by understanding that countries have agreed to attempt to limit global warming to a certain amount (1.5°C above preindustrial levels) to avoid the most severe impacts of climate change. Reaching this target would require countries to immediately and drastically reduce greenhouse gas emissions and also use technologies that aim to remove carbon dioxide from the atmosphere, called **carbon dioxide removal**.[39]

But right now, the world is already on track to overshoot, or surpass the internationally agreed-upon targets for slowing climate change. This is because countries are not taking enough steps to reduce greenhouse gas emissions. The world is still increasing the amount of carbon dioxide in the atmosphere.

Also, removing enough carbon dioxide from the atmosphere is expected to be challenging and costly. Some carbon dioxide removal approaches are only ideas currently, while others are in early stages of development. We still don't know

---

[38] Tilmes et al. (2022)   [39] Calvin et al. (2023).

whether, and how quickly, carbon dioxide removal technologies will be able to remove large amounts of carbon dioxide from the atmosphere – enough to reduce climate impacts over this century. It is extremely unlikely that carbon dioxide removal technologies will be able to remove enough carbon dioxide in time to help the Earth avoid surpassing the 1.5°C goal.[40]

As a result, scientists expect the planet will warm above our intended target in this decade.[41] The more global temperatures increase, the more exposed humans and other life on the planet are to dire risk of harm.

In this context, proponents argue that we need to explore whether SG could be used to help avoid the worst consequences of climate change.[42] Some of these proponents also argue that though solar geoengineering carries risks, those risks might be less than the risks of *not* using or researching this technology in a world with severe climate change impacts.[43]

Current research shows that SG could reduce some of the risks posed by climate change if used responsibly.[44] Scientists estimate that using solar geoengineering to reflect about 1 percent of all incoming sunlight would offset all of the warming caused so far by elevated carbon dioxide levels.[45] Reflecting less sunlight may still significantly reduce climate impacts.

As already discussed, solar geoengineering cannot solve climate change alone. So proponents envision using solar geoengineering along with other strategies to help stave off the worst effects of climate change. One widely discussed scenario would be to use SG temporarily to reduce climate impacts while states ramp up emission reductions and CDR.[46] Under this proposal, SG is used as a **stopgap** measure, which is a tool that does not fully resolve a problem but is proposed as a way to buy time for the development of solutions that would.[47]

You can see how this might help in Figure 9. This diagram shows how SG could be deployed for a limited period of time to prevent climate impacts from worsening, buying time for countries to reduce greenhouse gas emissions and remove carbon dioxide from the atmosphere. The "business as usual" line shows how climate impacts will worsen if we continue to fail to respond to climate change. The "cut emissions aggressively" line shows how sharp emission reductions would prevent climate impacts from rising further; however, this cannot reduce them because concentrations of greenhouse gasses remain too high. The

---

[40] Wieners et al. (2023)   [41] Hansen et al. 2023.; Calvin et al. (2023)

[42] "An Open Letter Regarding Research on Reflecting Sunlight to Reduce the Risks of Climate Change." n.d. Climate Intervention Research Letter. Accessed May 30, 2024. https://climate-intervention-research-letter.org/.

[43] Wieners et al. (2023)

[44] Keith and Irvine (2016); Irvine et al. (2019); Parson and Keith (2024)

[45] Irvine et al. (2019); NASEM (2021).   [46] MacMartin et al. (2018)   [47] Buck et al. (2020)

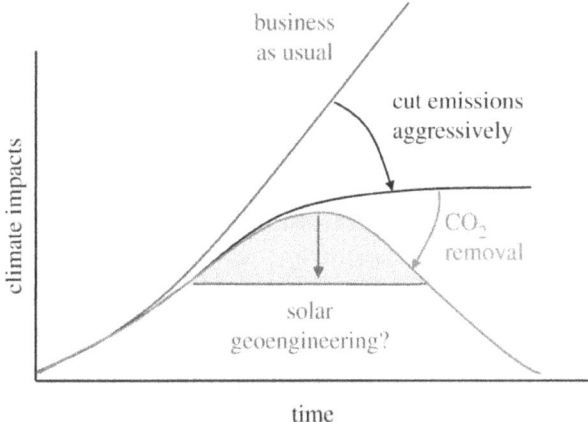

Figure 9 The use of solar geoengineering as a stopgap measure in an overshoot scenario

Source: Used with permission of The Royal Society (UK), from Solar geoengineering as part of an overall strategy for meeting the 1.5°C Paris target, by Keith, David W; MacMartin, Douglas G; Ricke, Katharine L, Volume 376, 2018. Permission conveyed through Copyright Clearance Center, Inc. This content is licensed by The Royal Society (UK), and is NOT part of the Gold Open Access license.

"CO_2 removal" line shows how removing carbon dioxide *alongside* aggressive emissions cuts can reduce climate impacts over time because concentrations of greenhouse gasses eventually are lowered. While this would lead to a return to a safe climate in the long term, temperatures are still likely to surpass temperature targets for a period of time, called the **overshoot** period. The gray shaded shape and blue arrow show how solar geoengineering could temporarily reduce severe climate impacts during the overshoot period.

Most scientists agree that we do not currently know whether the benefits of such an approach would outweigh its risks and harms, leading some to advocate for more research to help us make informed decisions.[48] Opponents of further research argue that devoting time and resources to this research would take momentum away from efforts to reduce greenhouse gas emissions, and that decisions about this technology would not be made in ways that are democratic and include developing countries.[49]

Many people who advocate for solar geoengineering research share these concerns, but generally believe the benefits of pursuing research outweigh the risk of harm, and that it could be possible to include developing countries in research and decision-making (Section 7).

---

[48] Wieners et al. (2023)   [49] Biermann et al. (2022)

6.5 What Do We Know about Solar Geoengineering, and What Do We Not Know?

In this section, we explain what researchers who study solar geoengineering have found. But it's important to note that these studies still leave many questions unanswered. Research on volcanic eruptions and marine clouds goes back several decades, and the past two decades have seen a large increase in the use of climate and atmospheric modeling research to study the potential impacts of SG. However, our efforts to understand how the climate would respond to SG and in turn how these climate impacts would affect people and the environment have been very limited. Moreover, the exact climate impact for each method would depend on how it is used and where it is deployed. This makes it difficult to make broad statements about SG impacts that are always true.

Scientists are confident that research will help reduce some of these uncertainties, and provide valuable knowledge that can help society make informed decisions about solar geoengineering.

Resolving some uncertainties would require scientists and others to study solar geoengineering outside of a lab, in the real world, in what experts usually refer to as "outdoor experiments." For some uncertainties, outdoor experiments would need to be conducted on a large scale and over a long period of time – making such an activity indistinguishable from a deployment, where the technology is used to cool the planet or a region, rather than just for research.[50]

In effect, this means that it is impossible to have full certainty about the global impacts of a solar geoengineering deployment before deployment takes place.[51] Any decisions related to whether and how to deploy the technology; to maintain or modify an existing solar geoengineering deployment; and to end a deployment would all involve risks and uncertainties. Deciding not to deploy the technology involves risks too. These decisions may be made in the future when the impacts of climate change are even worse than they are now.

6.5.1 Atmospheric Impacts and Climate Response

Solar geoengineering would decrease global average temperatures.[52] This means that, according to existing research, the technology would likely reduce many, if not most, climate impacts and risks for many people.[53]

However, the cooling effect would not be the same across the world, and solar geoengineering would not exactly reverse climate change, meaning some changes in temperature and precipitation would remain relative to a world

---

[50] MacMartin et al. (2016)   [51] MacMartin et al. (2016)   [52] E.g., Irvine et al. (2016)
[53] Keith and Irvine (2016)

that had neither increased greenhouse gasses nor solar geoengineering.[54] How large these remaining changes in temperature and precipitation are depends on which geoengineering method is used and how it is used. Solar geoengineering may also change how much temperatures rise and lower with the seasons. Regions closer to poles, for example, may experience warmer winters and cooler summers.

Just as SG would not fully reverse all the temperature changes caused by climate change, it would not reverse all the precipitation changes, or changes to events such as rainfall and snowfall. SG would alter the **hydrological cycle**, or water cycle, which refers to how water moves from the atmosphere to the Earth's surface and then back again through processes of evaporation, condensation, precipitation, transpiration, and runoff. Even if SG were used to restore global temperatures to 1990 levels, it would create a new climate with slightly different precipitation patterns.[55] On a global level, scientists know that SG using stratospheric aerosol injection or marine cloud brightening would lower global precipitation levels in proportion with temperature, meaning that more cooling would lead to lower levels of precipitation. However on a regional level, impacts on the water cycle are more difficult to predict. Regional impacts on the water cycle depend on which solar geoengineering technology is used and how, making it difficult to say whether those changes would be harmful or beneficial.[56]

The Indian and East Asian monsoons are expected to gain intensity under climate change, meaning they are expected to deliver much larger amounts of rain than they do today. Monsoons are seasonal shifts in wind directions that often cause a very rainy or dry season. Several studies suggest some deployments of SAI could weaken the Indian and East Asian monsoons relative to today.[57] Some MCB studies show more complex results, showing that the technology would increase precipitation over India.[58] Overall, research suggests that, in comparison to a planet that is warmed by greenhouse gasses, SAI would generally reduce precipitation on land, and also decrease extreme weather events, such as heavy rainfall, flooding, and drought.[59] Otherwise, the impacts of solar geoengineering on the hydrological cycle appear to depend heavily on the SG method used and the region studied.

Some aerosols, including sulfate, also absorb longwave radiation, which cause warming in the lower stratosphere in tropical regions. This small heating effect slightly offsets some of the cooling effects of aerosols resulting from their reflectivity, requiring the addition of more aerosol material to compensate for

[54] Ricke et al. (2010)   [55] Irvine et al. (2016)   [56] Ricke et al. (2023)
[57] Tilmes et al. (2013); Ricke et al. (2023); Bal et al. (2019); Bhowmick et al. (2021)
[58] Jones et al. (2009)   [59] Tilmes et al. (2013)

the warming. However, scientists do not currently know how much warming would occur.

SG might also impact the atmosphere in other ways. For example, SAI using sulfate material might impact the ozone in the stratosphere, which shields the planet from harmful ultraviolet radiation. Scientists are trying to better understand whether and how much SAI would impact this ozone.

Additionally, stratospheric aerosols scatter sunlight. This causes more sunlight to hit the planet's surface at angles rather than directly, which may impact plant growth. It would also very slightly "whiten" the appearance of the sky.

6.5.2 Environmental and Ecological Impacts

Because solar geoengineering would change Earth's temperature and precipitation, it could also affect a wide range of natural systems that sustain life on the planet. More research is needed to better understand the potential impacts of SG on, for example, biodiversity, the health of biological communities, plant growth, crop production, fishery production, ice loss and sea level rise, wildfire risks, predator–prey dynamics, and more.

For instance, researchers don't yet know how solar geoengineering could affect **vegetation**, or plant life. This is important because plants also provide homes for most animals and provide food and other resources for humans. Solar geoengineering could alter how much sunlight and water are available to plants to help them grow. For stratospheric aerosol injection using sulfur, plants may also be impacted by more acidic soils in some regions due to increased acid rain.[60]

Some studies also show that solar geoengineering could alter how the molecule carbon moves throughout the planet and all living things. Solar geoengineering would likely raise the amount of carbon absorbed by ecosystems on land and in the ocean and slightly reduce the amount of carbon that exists in the air in the form of carbon dioxide.[61] But if the ocean absorbs more carbon, it may make ocean acidification worse (Section 4).

Scientists expect that solar geoengineering would also affect the ocean in several other ways, including impacts on its chemistry, nutrients, and oxygen. Some studies show that (relative to a warmer world without SG) SG could decrease what scientists call **net primary productivity** in the ocean, which is the production of organic matter by small plants called phytoplankton, and which is a critical part of the ocean food chain.[62]

Scientists also don't know how much solar geoengineering could lower sea levels worldwide. Climate change causes sea level to rise in two ways: by

---

[60] Visioni et al. (2020)   [61] Cao and Jiang (2017)   [62] Lauvset et al. (2017)

melting ice sheets, and by causing seawater to expand as it heats up (**thermal expansion**). By reducing surface temperatures, SG would likely reduce sea level rise by slowing thermal expansion of seawater and also likely by slowing the melting of ice sheets. However, many factors affect ice sheet loss, and ice sheets may start disappearing much more quickly than they are today as the planet warms. So scientists cannot yet predict whether solar geoengineering could actually reduce sea level very much.

Researchers also don't yet know how solar geoengineering could affect where plants and animals are able to live. Climate change is already causing some species to go extinct and others to leave their homes in search of new places where they can survive. One study found that solar geoengineering could stop or even reverse this climate-driven migration.[63] But it also found that if we then suddenly stopped using solar geoengineering, species might be forced to migrate even faster than under climate change alone. Overall, much more research is needed to understand how SG would impact species' migration and extinction.

6.5.3 Human Society and Health

Solar geoengineering could affect humans and our well-being, and it carries both risks and potential benefits for people. For instance, solar geoengineering could trigger changes that directly affect human health, and it could also alter environmental systems that we depend on for our survival, including agriculture, water availability, and biological communities that include plants, animals and other life forms.[64] But researchers haven't studied these issues very much, and therefore do not thoroughly understand how solar geoengineering would impact our lives overall.[65]

For instance, solar geoengineering could have complex effects on our health. Climate change has harmful impacts on human health and mortality due to more frequent and intense heat waves, increased spread of some types of infectious diseases, and worse air pollution due to higher temperatures.[66] Since solar geoengineering would reduce temperatures and heatwaves, deaths associated with higher temperatures would decline.[67] But if we inject sulfur, for example, into the atmosphere to cool the planet, this sulfur would eventually fall to the Earth's surface, creating potential health hazards from exposure to the material.[68] Fallen sulfur aerosol material would slightly worsen air quality and cause increases in respiratory disease rates.[69] And sulfate material might also impact the protective ozone layer, which could lead to more exposure to the

---

[63] Trisos et al. (2018)   [64] Irvine et al. (2017)   [65] Irvine et al. (2017)   [66] USGCRP (2018)
[67] Eastham et al. (2018); Harding et al. (2024)   [68] Eastham (2015)   [69] Eastham et al. (2018)

harmful ultraviolet radiation that causes skin cancer.[70] However, some researchers think that these health risks are small compared to the number of lives that solar geoengineering could save by slowing climate change.[71]

Solar geoengineering may also change how people in different regions are exposed to infectious diseases, each of which thrives under certain temperatures. People in some regions could become more vulnerable to diseases such as malaria, whereas others could become less vulnerable, depending on how solar geoengineering changes local temperatures.[72]

As for climate change, SG may also change how people in different regions are exposed to infectious diseases, each of which thrives under certain temperatures. People in some regions could become more vulnerable to diseases such as malaria, whereas others become less vulnerable, depending on how much cooling is achieved and where.[73]

Finally, solar geoengineering could affect the crops that we grow for food. But we also do not know how exactly the technology would impact our global food supply. Crop production is sensitive to many factors related to temperature and rainfall that solar geoengineering would likely alter, and its impacts are likely to vary by crop and region.[74]

Overall, we have a limited understanding of SG impacts on human society and health, and more research would be needed to better understand how SG would affect people, our livelihoods, and our well-being.

6.6 Types of SG Research in the Near Term

Scientists have proposed using several types of research to better understand the potential impacts of SG. These include modeling, laboratory experiments, small-scale outdoor experiments, and observational studies. All types of research have different advantages and disadvantages for enhancing understanding, and they also carry different benefits, risks, and costs.

6.6.1 Atmospheric and Climate Models

Most of the existing research about SG uses computer models to understand how SG would impact the climate. These computer models use information about how the climate works to simulate what would happen if we do something to alter it. But for several reasons, computer models cannot precisely predict the effects of solar geoengineering. This is in part because models simplify important parts of the climate that work at smaller spatial and time scales than models normally simulate.

---

[70] Eastham et al. (2018)   [71] Eastham et al. (2018); Harding et al. (2024)
[72] Carlson et al. (2022)   [73] Carlson et al. (2022)
[74] E.g., Parkes et al. (2015); Yang et al. (2016); Grant et al. 2025.

Still, these models will always be a vital and important tool for studying SG. Crucially, they are the only way we can estimate how using solar geoengineering would create changes in our climate on a large scale. Scientists use data from laboratory settings, small scale-outdoor experiments, and observational studies to help make these models more accurate.

6.6.2 Laboratory Experiments

Scientists use laboratory experiments to study physical processes in a controlled environment. These experiments take place in specialized scientific facilities, and not outdoors. Laboratory experiments help to build better computer models by, for example, allowing scientists to learn about the chemistry of potential materials used for SAI, including how they interact with other gasses and material. Unlike in the outdoors, laboratory studies enable scientists to control certain conditions, which makes these experiments more useful. Laboratory experiments could also be used to conduct engineering tests of equipment that could be used to release aerosols. However, while laboratory experiments can provide measurements that inform computer models, the laboratory cannot fully capture the complexity of the Earth. For example, it is impossible to recreate the conditions of the stratosphere – the area where we would perform stratospheric aerosol injection – for more than a few minutes. So we cannot use laboratory experiments to learn about how this intervention might evolve over months.

6.6.3 Small-scale Outdoor Experiments

Studies of how SG would work in the real world, where SG would actually be used, would help provide even more confidence in the accuracy of model and laboratory studies. Outdoor experiments, also called field experiments, include scientific research activity that occurs outside of the confines of a computer or a laboratory. Scientists and some private sector actors have proposed several different forms of outdoor experiments, including some for testing devices that could be used to spray sulfur or sea salt into the air, and others for testing how well these particles reflect sunlight in the real world. Some experiments might aim to create and study a cooling effect whereas others would not. Some experiments proposed so far would occur on a small scale, by impacting an area no larger than a sports field. In contrast to large-scale experiments, which aim to test the climate effects of solar geoengineering on certain regions or even on the entire planet, small-scale experiments would not have any physical impact on regional or global climate.

Some experiments could study the physics and chemistry of aerosols. For example, the Stratospheric Controlled Perturbation Experiment (SCoPEx) proposed by a team of researchers at Harvard University would have measured how a small amount of mineral dust (calcium carbonate), injected into the air interacts with other particles in the atmosphere.[75] A specialized balloon would have released a small amount of material into the air and measurement equipment on the balloon would have measured how these materials moved through the air, affected the chemistry of the air, and scattered light. The experiment would not have achieved any climate impact. Scientists have previously conducted environmental science experiments unrelated to solar geoengineering that also release materials outdoors.

6.6.4 Observational Studies

Studies that compare model results to observations of similar processes in the real world, such as volcanic eruptions or the impact of ship exhaust on marine clouds, can also help provide confidence in the accuracy of climate models. Observational studies can gather data using various forms of measurement equipment, sometimes using specialized balloon platforms and satellites. If a model predicts impacts that are in line with what occurred in the real world, and it does so for the right reasons, we can feel more confident that the model can usefully predict important physical processes.

Observational studies can also be used to better understand natural and physical processes that SG would alter. For instance, scientists might conduct an observational study to examine how many small particles already exist in the stratosphere, or how existing aerosols in the lower atmosphere interact with clouds. They could use information from these studies to improve computer models.

Importantly, observational studies do not aim to introduce new aerosol material into the atmosphere, nor do they aim to achieve any climate impact. For example, the United States National Oceanic and Atmospheric Administration (NOAA) is currently using a high-altitude airplane equipped with scientific measurement equipment to study what aerosols are currently in different parts of the atmosphere, how they are transported around the globe, and how they reflect sunlight.

Overall, a combination of modeling, laboratory and field experiments, and observational studies is likely to provide the best approach to gaining confidence in our ability to predict the impacts of any proposed use of solar geoengineering. Scientists can use laboratory and outdoor experiments and observational studies to verify and improve models, which are then used to

---

[75] "Keutsch Group at Harvard – SCoPEx." n.d. Accessed February 7, 2024. www.keutschgroup .com/scopex.

understand and assess how SG might affect the climate, the environment, and people. Some social scientists suggest that other forms of research, including methods that collect information from people, such as interviews and surveys, would also be needed to fully understand the potential impact of solar geoengineering on people, their well-being, and their livelihoods.[76] Some argue that other ways of knowing and producing knowledge about the world, such as those used by Indigenous Peoples, would be needed as well.

7 Solar Geoengineering Governance and Policy

7.1 Introduction

As solar geoengineering (SG) has been increasingly researched and discussed as a potential climate response option, much of this discussion and research has focused on governance and policy. **Governance** is a broad term that refers to all the activities, processes, and rules that guide behavior and decision-making in a particular issue area.[77] Governance includes both formal regional, national, and international laws and policies imposed by governments and international organizations, as well as informal rules or guidelines that influence people's actions and behavior, such as voluntary codes of conduct. In the context of SG, governance can influence how SG is researched and whether and how it could be deployed.[78] This section provides an overview of the SG governance discussion, and it also covers the limited efforts so far to govern SG in practice. While there has been a lot of discussion and debate about establishing governance of SG, a **governance gap** remains, as existing rules, policies, and institutions do not fully address the risks and issues associated with SG.

There are two main areas of discussion around solar geoengineering governance. The first relates to SG **research**, which includes activities that aim to produce knowledge about solar geoengineering technologies. The second is SG **deployment**, which refers to using solar geoengineering techniques to intentionally change the climate of a region or of the entire planet. We also distinguish between indoor and outdoor research, where **indoor** research includes modeling studies and experiments using laboratory equipment, and **outdoor** research involves field tests and experiments to study or test SG technologies and its potential impacts in the real world, outside of a lab.[79] Some outdoor research might have a physical impact on the immediate surrounding area of an experiment, but when we talk about "deployment," we mean solar geoengineering activities that would have far wider impacts and would affect many regions and countries, and likely the entire world.

---

[76] Hourdequin (2019); Stilgoe (2016)   [77] Chhetri et al. (2018); Florini and Sovacool (2009)
[78] Chhetri et al. (2018).   [79] For a more in-depth discussion see Parker (2014).

Much of the discussion on solar geoengineering governance revolves around questions about how, when, by whom, and where SG research and deployment should be governed. Should we only govern solar geoengineering deployment, or should we also govern research that carries physical risks, such as large outdoor experiments? Should we also govern smaller outdoor research projects and/or indoor research? Should we make laws to govern solar geoengineering, or would voluntary forms of governance be sufficient? Should we make decisions about solar geoengineering through existing international institutions, or should we create new institutions to address the challenges unique to solar geoengineering? Should decisions about SG be made alongside other decisions about climate change, or should the issues be kept separate? Should these decisions ultimately be made by technical experts and government officials, or should the public have a role in making decisions too? These are some of the many questions that have been discussed and debated so far.

7.2 Why Govern Solar Geoengineering?

It's important to consider different reasons why SG should be governed in the first place. Most people who have studied the issue agree that governance is needed to understand, reduce, and/or eliminate various potential risks associated with solar geoengineering.[80] For example, most experts agree we need to develop governance to prevent unauthorized or **rogue deployments**, where one or more actors deploy solar geoengineering without gaining formal approval to do so from governments or international bodies, or even in the face of opposition from other countries. Governance is also needed to detect and deter irresponsible forms of research that pose significant or unnecessary risk.

Some experts are also concerned that disagreements over whether and how to deploy solar geoengineering could create conflict, potentially threatening international peace and security. Others are concerned that attention toward SG may reduce the world's resolve to reduce greenhouse gas emissions, a phenomenon known as the **moral hazard** concern. Another prominent concern is that beginning research could create a **slippery slope** that makes deployment more likely because research might make the idea more widely accepted, or create groups that are invested in developing the technology further.[81] Some experts are also concerned by different forms of **technological lock-in**, whereby the decisions we make about solar geoengineering now restrict the options available to future generations, or whereby society embraces one particular form of solar geoengineering, even though other techniques may actually work better.[82]

---

[80] Jinnah (2018)   [81] Tang (2023)   [82] Cairns (2014); Lin (2020)

Most experts agree that we need to develop some form of solar geoengineering governance to address these risks and issues.

Right now, experts are debating the purpose of solar geoengineering research governance. We can place their ideas on a spectrum, from *restricting* to *enabling* research.[83]

On one end of the spectrum, some experts argue that governance is needed to **restrict** solar geoengineering research and potential future use. For instance, some experts propose to ban the development of solar geoengineering technologies and even some research, particularly outdoor experiments. These experts argue that solar geoengineering is unnecessary, highly risky, and dangerous, and that considering this technology would damage international efforts to reduce greenhouse gas emissions and adapt to climate impacts. These experts want governance to discourage consideration of solar geoengineering and restrict or ban outdoor research and any deployment.[84]

On the other end of the spectrum, some experts argue that governance should **enable** the potential future use of SG, including by funding and approving solar geoengineering research, and allow outdoor experiments.[85] These experts argue that solar geoengineering may play a critical role in humanity's response to climate change, as it appears likely that mitigation, adaptation, and carbon removal will not be enough to prevent severe climate change. Experts who make this argument say that we need to use governance to ensure that scientific research can move forward and that this research is transparent, avoids creating harmful impacts, and does not take attention away from mitigation and adaptation, which are the most important tools.

7.3 How to Govern Solar Geoengineering?

There are many reasons to govern solar geoengineering. But how might we do this? And who might be involved?

Many experts argue that we should use collaborative, participatory, flexible, and forward-looking approaches to govern issues and technologies that carry significant risks, uncertainties, and controversy. *Collaborative* approaches include coordinating with multiple actors, including local, national, regional, and global government bodies and other groups. *Participatory* approaches include involving the public and interested groups that could be affected by the technology. *Flexible* forms of governance can adjust and respond to changes in knowledge and circumstances. Finally, forward-looking, or *anticipatory*,

---

[83] Gupta et al. (2020) [84] Biermann et al. (2022); Gupta et al. (2024) [85] Gupta et al. (2020)

forms of governance are attentive to what might happen in the future and how conditions might change.[86]

The following is a discussion of several governance mechanisms that governance experts have proposed, with a focus on mechanisms proposed to govern SG *research* in the near future. **Governance mechanisms** are tools that a wide variety of actors and groups use to achieve governance goals.

Governance principles provide high-level guidelines that are intended to guide behavior, including solar geoengineering research, development, and any future potential deployment. Some are also intended to inform the development of more specific and concrete governance mechanisms. Several sets of principles have been proposed by experts, including the Oxford Principles, which were developed by a group of five social and legal scholars.[87] In no order of importance, the Oxford Principles are to:

1. Regulate geoengineering in the public interest by appropriate national and/ or international bodies;
2. Require those conducting geoengineering research to notify, consult, and ideally obtain the prior informed consent of those affected by research activities;
3. Completely disclose all research plans and openly publish all research results;
4. Assess (evaluate) the environmental and social impacts of geoengineering research by appropriate independent national, regional, or international bodies;
5. Make decisions about deployment only after robust governance procedures are already in place.[88]

To provide more specific guidance, experts have developed codes of conduct. A **code of conduct** is a set of voluntary rules and guidelines that researchers, research funders, and/or scientific agencies agree to follow when planning, funding, and conducting solar geoengineering research. For example, in consultation with other academics, policymakers, and other interested groups, a legal scholar developed a Code of Conduct for Responsible Geoengineering Research.[89] The code provides concrete guidance about research governance on how to, for example:

- Prevent environmental harm from outdoor experiments;
- Provide public information about research – particularly outdoor experiments;
- Provide advance notice to the public about research, and allow the public to comment on it, and;
- Promote knowledge sharing and international cooperation in research.

---

[86] Guston (2014)   [87] Rayner et al. (2013)   [88] Rayner et al. (2013)   [89] Hubert (2021)

Several governance mechanisms are designed to promote transparency and knowledge sharing about solar geoengineering research. Transparency is important because it can help people understand the risks and benefits of solar geoengineering, promote legitimate and accountable decision-making, help people trust actors who study and govern the technology, and boost international cooperation.[90] Governance mechanisms to support transparency include creating publicly accessible **clearinghouses**, which are databases that contain information related to solar geoengineering research, including information about proposed projects or experiments, who is funding the research, and research data and results.[91] No such clearinghouse exists for solar geoengineering, and there are many different ways to design one. Countries could create clearinghouses about research that happens within their borders, and these clearinghouses could be linked to larger regional or international clearinghouses. Additionally, countries and researchers could either volunteer or be required to contribute to these databases, which could include information about only outdoor experiments, or any form of solar geoengineering research.

Various forms of assessments and reviews are also important governance mechanisms that can help bring transparency to solar geoengineering activities, promote public trust in research, and enable consideration of multiple forms of risks in decision-making. **Assessments** and **reviews** are processes in which a group studies an ongoing or proposed activity to identify and evaluate its impacts. Ideally, research assessments would be undertaken by an independent body composed of experts from a broad range of relevant backgrounds and representatives from communities that would be affected by the research.[92] Such bodies could assess individual research projects or experiments, multiple programs or policies, or they could create a comprehensive assessment of all solar geoengineering research activities.

Moreover, assessments can consider physical impacts as well as social, economic, and other nonphysical impacts, such as ethical challenges. Assessments can also include public comment and input into the assessment process to incorporate public knowledge and foster transparency of risks. For example, an independent advisory body to a canceled solar geoengineering research experiment, which had been proposed by a team at Harvard University, designed an assessment process that included reviewing the experiment's engineering safety, scientific merit, funding, regulatory and legal compliance, and the perspectives of society.[93]

---

[90] Callies (2019); Craik and Moore (2014)   [91] Craik and Moore (2014)   [92] NASEM (2021)
[93] Jinnah et al. (2024)

Permits are likely to play an important role in governing SG research and can help minimize risk of harm and assure the public research is being conducted in a responsible manner. A **permit** is a legally authorized permission to conduct an activity that would otherwise not be allowed.[94] These may be issued in the form of general permits that authorize multiple activities, or specific permits that only authorize a single experiment, for example. Depending on the potential risks, different types of SG research may be subject to different types of permits.[95] A permitting approval process could require the applicant to take steps to, for example, notify the public about the experiment and minimize harm in order to be granted permission to proceed. Currently, many countries, including the United States, lack a permitting system that would apply to SG research.[96]

Intellectual property laws and protections can shape incentives to research and develop SG technologies and can also restrict who has access to data and innovations. While SG researchers have so far practiced open access to research and sharing of data, that may change, particularly if commercial actors become involved in research.[97] Coordinated efforts on national and international levels could facilitate access to patented innovations and discourage patent holders from enforcing patents against researchers seeking access.[98]

A variety of governance mechanisms could facilitate **international cooperation** in research, whereby research programs include researchers from multiple countries, and where research efforts occurring within different countries are coordinated. International cooperation is important for helping to ensure that all countries have access to and benefit from SG research, enabling all countries to make informed decisions about it and helping to minimize domination by powerful countries. Funders could choose to prioritize projects that include international teams and partnerships, or for certain projects, they may require that researchers from multiple countries are included.[99] Additionally, national scientific or research organizations could coordinate research programs with other countries, including those that do not have national SG research programs. They could do so by, for example, publishing joint calls for research proposals, sharing information on national programs and best practices, and providing support to research teams in developing countries.[100]

Capacity building efforts can also help facilitate international cooperation and ensure that developing countries and communities that are disproportionately vulnerable to climate change are able to participate and play leading roles in SG discussion, research, and decision-making. **Capacity building** refers to a process of strengthening a community or country's ability to achieve goals or

---

[94] Biber and Ruhl (2014)   [95] NASEM (2021)   [96] NASEM (2021)
[97] Reynolds et al. (2017)   [98] NASEM (2021)   [99] Chhetri et al. (2018)
[100] NASEM (2021)

accomplish tasks, such as creating effective mechanisms to govern SG research. Capacity building can take many different forms, and can involve a wide variety of activities and tools. One example of a capacity building mechanism is the Degrees Modelling Fund, which provides research grants and mentorship to teams in developing countries to study the potential impacts of solar geoengineering in their region, and to ultimately ensure that developing countries can use their own expertise to make decisions.[101]

Finally, most people think that the public should be involved in creating research programs that are publicly acceptable and provide useful information for decision-making.[102] **Public engagement** can come in many different forms, and people in different countries sometimes prefer to participate in different ways.[103] It generally involves an invitation to local or national groups or communities to participate in an activity related to learning about, discussing, or even making decisions about SG and its research or deployment.

Figure 10 illustrates some different forms of public engagement mapped on two spectrums. Public engagement can increase public trust in a research program or governing body and improve the research by incorporating public information and values. Many argue that because solar geoengineering would affect everyone in potentially significant ways, public engagement is the right thing to do.[104]

Public engagement could occur within individual research projects or within a broader national or international research program, although experts disagree about when and where public engagement must be done, as it takes a lot of money and time, and it's difficult to do well. Though it is not yet widely practiced, multiple public engagement activities on solar geoengineering have been completed. For example, a proposed SG-related outdoor experiment in the United Kingdom, called the SPICE project, used several deliberative workshops with members of the public to better understand what the public thought about the experiment, and whether they might support it.[105]

Importantly, none of these governance mechanisms can sufficiently govern all aspects of SG alone. It is important to consider how these governance mechanisms might work together to form a governance framework, where multiple governance mechanisms are deployed simultaneously and linked together.[106]

---

[101] "Degrees Research Funds." n.d. The DEGREES Initiative (website). Accessed February 6, 2024. www.degrees.ngo/degrees-research-funds/.

[102] Fritz et al. (2024)   [103] Fritz et al. (2024)   [104] Fiorino (1990); Flegal et al. (2019).

[105] Pidgeon et al. 2013.

[106] For an example of a comprehensive governance framework for a specific proposed research experiment, the SCoPEX Advisory Committee developed a governance framework that includes five focus areas of review, including an engineering safety review, scientific merit review, financial review, legal review, and societal review. See Jinnah et al. 2024.

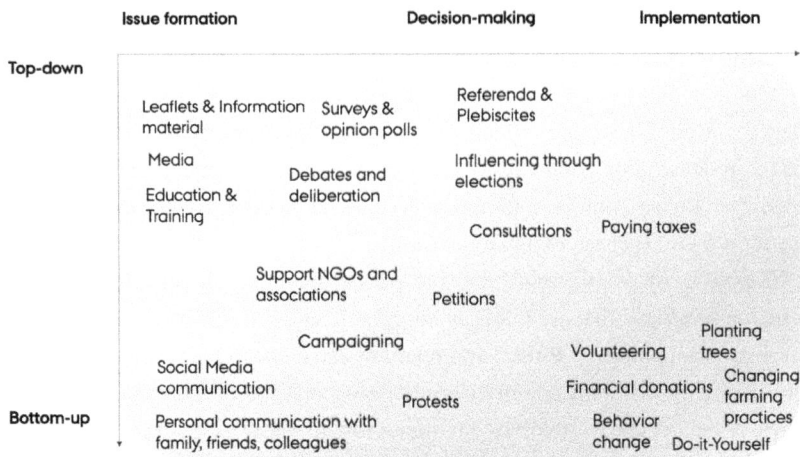

Figure 10 Different forms of public engagement. The figure is adapted from Fritz et al. (2024).[107]

For example, in 2021 the United States National Academies of Sciences, Engineering and Medicine (NASEM) recommended that the United States create a research program in coordination with other countries, and also create a governance framework, in which solar geoengineering research and governance are mutually supportive. This is because SG research, including on its social, political, legal, and ethical dimensions, can help inform how governance can and should develop to be most effective, and governance can in turn help advance and steer research toward socially beneficial ends.[108] The NASEM's proposed governance framework includes continuous mechanisms for engagement with the public and with other interested groups in relevant parts of the program's research and governance. Moreover, regular assessments of the program by experts and interested groups would be conducted to ensure the program is still needed and to update its goals in response to new findings or developments. Importantly, the program would create **exit ramps**, which are sets of criteria and processes for ending research activity if it appears to be too risky or unlikely to work.[109]

The previously discussed governance mechanisms are not the only possible ones, and new ideas could be developed. Some emphasize that creating SG governance should be a process that includes awareness, discussion, and engagement from members of the public, experts of different disciplines, government officials, and civil society.[110]

---

[107] We adapted this figure from Fritz et al. 2024. Specifically, we cropped Figure 2 in Fritz et al. (2024) to include only Figure 2(B). This figure was reproduced under a CC BY 4.0 license. To view a copy of this license, visit http://creativecommons.org/licenses/by/4.0/.
[108] See NASEM (2021) Sec. 3.3b.   [109] NASEM (2021)   [110] Hubert (2021)

7.4 Existing Forms of Governance Relevant to Solar Geoengineering

In addition to proposed governance mechanisms and frameworks that are intended to govern SG research, there are also currently existing governance mechanisms that experts argue are applicable to SG research, but that were not created with SG in mind. **Hard law** refers to legally binding principles, national laws, and international treaties that countries enforce within their own jurisdictions, or in the case of international treaties, that countries agree to comply with. Many countries have **national laws** that are likely to apply to some SG research activities, such as environmental regulations and intellectual property law.

Several **international treaties**, which are agreements between countries that govern countries' rights, duties, and obligations, are also likely to apply to some SG research activity, and SG has been addressed within international negotiations surrounding several treaties. Countries that agree to follow the requirements of a treaty are called **parties** to the treaty. Parties to the *London Convention/London Protocol*, which regulates marine pollution caused by ships dumping material at sea, recently adopted an amendment that includes a regulatory framework for SG activities that would affect the marine environment. But countries are not yet legally required to follow this framework, because too few of them have agreed to it.[111] Moreover, in 2010, parties to the *Convention on Biological Diversity,* which governs how countries protect and use ecosystems, passed a resolution suggesting that "no climate-related geoengineering activities that may affect biodiversity take place" until there's an "adequate scientific basis" on which to justify such activities and assessment of risks has occurred, with the exception of "small scale scientific studies."[112] The resolution is not legally binding, however, meaning that no one is legally required to follow it.

Several other international treaties are also likely to apply to certain SG activities. The *Montreal Protocol* requires parties to reduce or prevent activities that would damage the ozone layer, which protects the planet from harmful ultraviolet radiation. The Montreal Protocol is relevant to SG because some materials proposed for stratospheric aerosol injection might also damage the ozone layer (Section 6). Additionally, the Convention on the Prohibition of Military or any other Hostile Use of Environmental Modification Techniques, or the *ENMOD Convention*, would prohibit countries from using SG to damage the environments of other countries.[113] Moreover, whereas the *United Nations*

---

[111] Burns and Talati (2025)

[112] COP. 2019. Convention on Biological Diversity, COP 10 Decision X(33) (2010), www.cbd.int/decision/cop/?id=12299

[113] Burns and Talati (2025)

Framework Convention on Climate Change (UNFCCC) and the *Paris Agreement* currently govern how countries avoid dangerous climate change primarily through mitigation and adaptation, parties could choose to address SG more directly through these agreements. Several aspects of the agreements might also apply, such as requirements to cooperate on climate-related research and avoid and minimize displacement due to climate impacts.[114]

7.5 International Dimensions of Solar Geoengineering and Its Governance

The international dimensions of SG and its potential impact on international relations and world politics have been widely discussed. Any attempt to deploy solar geoengineering, and in particular stratospheric aerosol injection, would impact the climate of the entire globe. Yet it could be deployed by a single country or potentially by a wealthy non-state actor, such as a large corporation. This is the crux of what's been called the **free-driver problem**, where SG may be cheap enough that one country decides to deploy it.[115] However, such a deployment may harm other countries. Further, even if all countries agreed to support a SG deployment program, countries have different ideas about what sort of climate would be best. As the world experiences more severe impacts from climate change, many experts are concerned that these challenges could lead to additional sources of international disagreement, conflict, and possibly even war.[116]

The international implications of SG have prompted much dialogue about the need to develop international governance arrangements that facilitate international dialogue, collective decision-making, and conflict management. Within the past two years, SG has been discussed and assessed within various international fora including:

- the United Nations Environment Program, which released an independent expert-led report on SG science and governance in 2023;[117]
- the United Nations Environment Assembly, which considered a resolution calling for an expert assessment of SG in 2019 and 2024. The resolution was withdrawn both times because countries could not agree on risks, framing, and activities;[118]
- the United Nations Human Rights Council, which released a report on the impact of SG and other new climate intervention technologies on human rights;[119]

---

[114] Craik and Burns (2019).   [115] Weitzman (2015).   [116] Dalby (2015).
[117] United Nations Environment Programme (2023)
[118] Jinnah and Nicholson (2019); Hassan (2024)
[119] United Nations Human Rights Council Advisory Committee (2023).

- the International Panel on Climate Change, which assessed SG within its Sixth Assessment Report (Section 4); and
- the United Nations Educational, Scientific, and Cultural Organization (UNESCO), which released a report on the ethics of climate engineering.[120]

Most of these efforts have included calls for effective and inclusive governance of SG research and deployment, intended in part to avoid threats to international peace and security. While much of the discussion has focused on the possibility that SG threatens international peace and security, some have proposed the possibility that SG could instead promote international cooperation and peace.[121]

While SG has recently entered mainstream discussions about climate policy and response, the world has yet to decide whether or how SG should be used to address climate change, including as a potential complement to mitigation, adaptation, and carbon removal. Right now, the important questions are whether different forms of SG research should proceed, and if so, how this research should be governed.

8 Solar Geoengineering Ethics and Justice

8.1 Introduction

As attention toward solar geoengineering (SG) as a potential climate response option has grown over the past two decades, much discussion has focused on whether considering, researching, or using this technology is the right thing to do. This section overviews the ethical issues surrounding SG, with a focus on challenges and possibilities related to justice.

But first, let's explain what we mean when we talk about ethics and justice. Let's start with **ethics**, which is a branch of philosophy concerned with the study of morality and moral values or principles. Morality considers what is right and wrong. Ethics are central to solar geoengineering, and we should study and seriously consider the ethical issues associated with its research and deployment.[122] Ethicists who study SG ask questions such as: What are the ethical challenges of SG? Could it be ethical to use solar geoengineering, and if so, how could we study or deploy the technology in a moral way?

Justice is concerned with the fair treatment of people and other living things. Justice is a broad concept that addresses many different types of concerns, including how decisions are made and how they impact different people and communities. Generally, justice could demand the protection of basic rights, the

---

[120] World Commission on the Ethics of Scientific Knowledge and Technology (COMEST) (2023)
[121] Buck (2022)   [122] Shepherd et al. (2009)

fair treatment of individuals and communities, and equal opportunity for all to participate in the decision-making processes that govern their lives.

Justice also addresses inequalities of power and advantage. Justice raises important and challenging issues for solar geoengineering. If the technology were able to relieve the suffering of billions of people, but it also causes some suffering by creating drought in some regions, what would justice require us to do? If everyone agreed to use solar geoengineering, would that make it just? What if some communities or countries disagreed? How should the interests of future generations and nonhuman species be respected and represented in decisions about solar geoengineering? If ethical compromises must be made, how should different options be compared? Who gets to decide which compromise is best?

8.2 Dimensions of Justice

There are many different ways to think about what is just or not. Ethicists identify multiple dimensions of justice, each of which brings attention to different concerns and questions. Each of these dimensions of justice can be applied to many issue areas to evaluate, for example, whether an action or policy is just or not.

For example, **distributive justice** is the demand for fairness in how the good and bad things in life are distributed.[123] Some of these things might include money, information, access to resources, basic rights, proximity to pollution, and more.[124] Distributive justice is concerned with who wins or loses from the way societies operate, and whether the benefits and costs of this are shared fairly between different individuals or groups of people.

Procedural justice is the demand for ensuring fairness when making decisions related to solar geoengineering research and deployment.[125] Procedural justice is concerned with power – with who has a seat at the table of decision-making, and particularly whether people who are affected by an action can participate fairly in deciding whether or how that action is taken.

Ethicists also emphasize the importance of **intergenerational justice**, which is the demand for fair distribution of benefits and burdens of solar geoengineering between current and future generations and respect for future generations' interests in decision-making.[126] Intergenerational justice is concerned with whether what we do now is fair to people who are not yet born, in terms of ensuring they are able to, for example, live a dignified life and make their own decisions about how they will live.

---

[123] Preston (2016)   [124] Sen (2011); Schlosberg and Carruthers (2010)   [125] Preston (2016)
[126] Svoboda et al. (2011); McKinnon (2019)

Ethicists also emphasize the importance of **recognitional justice**, which is related to people's identities. It requires "fairly representing and considering the cultures, values, and situations of all affected parties," thereby ensuring that people are acknowledged as equals.[127] In short, recognition is about treating people and their ideas with respect, so that diverse groups and individuals can truly engage as equals in decisions that affect them.[128] Procedural justice and recognitional justice are closely related. While procedural justice is concerned primarily with who has a seat at the table, recognitional justice is concerned with whether people and their ideas, values, and cultures are fairly considered and respected while they are at the table.

Additionally **restorative justice** requires that harms or wrongs done to people are repaired or restored. Restorative justice is concerned with empowering those who have been harmed or wronged to play an active role in the process of deciding how that harm or wrong should be repaired and with reconciliation between the perpetrators and victims of a harmful act.[129]

Rather than seeing these different forms of justice – distributive, procedural, intergenerational, and recognition, and restorative – as separate, many ethicists argue that each actually supports the others and all can be equally important for evaluating whether and how something is just.[130]

8.3 Climate Justice

Justice has long been a central concern in climate change discussion and politics. **Climate justice** is a set of interrelated ideas that apply the dimensions of justice discussed earlier to the specific issue of climate change. Climate justice could demand, for example, that poor communities and countries – especially those that have emitted less greenhouse gasses – should not be disproportionately impacted by climate change, and should play a leading role in determining how society responds to it.[131]

Concerns about climate justice often start from a concern that communities and countries that are most impacted by climate change are often the ones that have contributed the least to causing it. In other words, these communities and countries have historically emitted far less harmful greenhouse gasses than other countries that are more capable of facing climate change impacts. Vulnerable communities are also sometimes even harmed by attempts to address climate change, such as when carbon taxes are designed in ways that place greater financial burden on poorer households and communities.

---

[127] Whyte (2011, p. 200); see also Hourdequin (2019); Carr and Preston (2018)
[128] Fraser and Honneth (2003)   [129] Preston (2011); Forsyth et al. (2021)
[130] Schlosberg (2007); Hourdequin (2019).   [131] Schlosberg and Collins (2014); Caney (2005)

Importantly, a central notion of climate justice is that responses to climate change must not create new forms of injustice, or magnify existing forms of injustice or inequality. Moreover, rich countries who have contributed the most over time to causing climate change have greater resources available to adapt to its impacts, and greater political power to shape how humanity responds to the problem.

Other key concerns of climate justice include, for example, *inclusion* of affected communities in decision-making; *autonomy* of communities to decide their own climate response and future; *transparency* in how powerful actors impact the climate and respond to climate change; *compensation* for harms from climate change from rich countries to poor ones; and *sustainability* of society and the ecosystems humans depend on.[132]

A further, essential, dimension of climate justice is intergenerational. What we do now will impact future generations long after we are gone. How should we take account of the interests of future people in our present climate actions? How might we adjust our political institutions to do better in delivering justice to future people – especially people most vulnerable to climate impacts?[133]

8.4 Solar Geoengineering and Justice

What solar geoengineering means for climate justice remains a matter of debate. Some see the technology as a possible path toward reducing climate injustice. For example, if a deployment were to reduce harmful climate impacts on vulnerable communities, this might be just. Some argue that because SG currently appears capable of reducing climate harms that unfairly burden poor countries, rich countries are morally obligated to conduct research.[134]

Others think that solar geoengineering threatens climate justice. For example, if a rich country were to deploy SG on its own, or if research or deployment harms vulnerable communities, this would probably be unjust.

Some argue that it's not realistically possible to make democratic global decisions about solar geoengineering, and that poor communities and countries would not be equal partners in deciding whether to use SG. Others suggest that rather than arguing over what is best for poor communities and countries, these people should be empowered to make their own informed decisions about whether SG research is in their interest.[135] Even when concern for the autonomy and well-being of poor communities and countries is shared, there is disagreement about which is the right path forward.

---

[132] McKinnon (2022); Schlosberg and Collins (2014)
[133] Gardiner (2014); McKinnon (2011); Shue (2024)   [134] Horton and Keith (2016)
[135] Táíwò and Talati (2021)

SG presents many ethical challenges that relate directly to justice, making justice central to the discussions and debates surrounding SG.[136] This is due to two reasons.

First, SG approaches can potentially impact the entire global population, now and into the future (Section 6). Everyone is therefore impacted by decisions about whether and how to research or deploy SG. This raises the need for procedural justice by ensuring fairness in how decisions related to SG research and deployment are made.[137] Much of the discussion on procedural justice has focused on the need for participatory engagement in SG decision-making, so that decision-making procedures are inclusive in some way for all communities and countries. This is complicated by the fact that, although everyone has a stake in SG, not everyone is equally vulnerable to climate change – some communities and countries are more vulnerable than others, and therefore potentially have a greater stake in decisions about SG.[138] Procedural justice would also require governance mechanisms that deter actors from undertaking a deployment on their own or that participate in an illegal deployment (Section 7).[139]

The second reason why justice is such an integral part of the discussion surrounding SG is that the impacts of the technology are uncertain and are likely to be unevenly distributed (Section 6). This means that while most people may be better off under SG, some people may be worse off under SG, and this would likely include some communities that are already vulnerable to climate change, thereby compounding multiple injustices.[140] This raises the need for distributive justice through fairness in how the benefits and burdens of SG are distributed.[141] In the SG context, distributive justice also requires the need to avoid exacerbating existing injustices by taking steps to ensure communities and countries that are already vulnerable to climate change are not disproportionately harmed by SG's uneven impacts.[142] Distributive justice may also require some form of compensation for harm caused by SG.[143]

Issues related to intergenerational justice arise when we consider possible impacts of SG and of climate change on future generations. Climate change is expected to worsen throughout the century, and SG, if deployed, would need to be maintained until greenhouse gas concentrations return to safe levels (Section 6). Therefore, justice for future generations, who are not yet born and who cannot participate in decision-making, requires a fair distribution of the benefits and burdens of SG between current and future generations and respect for future generations' interests in decision-making.[144] Some justice

---

[136] Gardiner and Fragnière (2018); Preston (2016).   [137] Preston (2016)
[138] Svoboda et al. 2011.   [139] Svoboda et al. (2011).
[140] Preston (2012); Svoboda et al. (2011)   [141] Preston (2016).   [142] Preston (2012).
[143] Svoboda and Irvine (2014)   [144] Svoboda et al. (2011); McKinnon (2019)

experts also argue that it is not just humans that are deserving of justice; justice needs to account for all species, who are also impacted by human decisions and have moral value.[145]

Several ethicists argue that in addition to distributive, procedural, and inter-generational justice, the concept of recognition is critical to ensuring a just approach to SG research and governance. Recognition requires treating people and their ideas with respect, so that diverse groups and individuals can truly engage as equals in SG decision-making.[146] Special consideration is given to multiple groups of people.

First, recognition of the distinct approaches of Indigenous communities to governing, producing knowledge, and relating to nature is central to just approaches to researching and governing SG.[147] This requires that SG research and governance institutions recognize the sovereignty of Indigenous communities, as well as their position as already vulnerable to climate change in large part due to the long-term impacts of colonialism.[148] From this perspective, a just approach to considering SG would need to also include serious attention to reforms that aim to ensure Indigenous peoples can govern themselves as well as other topics and solutions that Indigenous communities value.[149] This requires that Indigenous peoples are not only "consulted" after decisions have been made, effectively negating their ability to influence how these decisions are made and undermining their autonomy.[150]

Additionally, because much of the research and discussion on SG has occurred in rich countries, special consideration within recognitional justice is given more broadly to inclusion of the diverse perspectives and values of communities and countries that are most affected by climate change and who have been marginalized from ongoing debates about how we should respond.[151] Overall, recognitional justice requires that any engagement in decision-making is *meaningful*, meaning participants are not only at the table, but they also have some influence over the process and outcome. That is, recognitional justice concerns redistributing power between vulnerable groups and those that have, historically, made them vulnerable.

Multiple other dimensions of justice could also inform what justice looks like in the SG context. For example, restorative justice may require mechanisms for compensation from any harm from SG research or deployment, and some could argue that SG is required as a way to repair the harm caused by climate change by restoring a safer climate.[152]

---

[145] Pellow (2017)   [146] Whyte (2012); Hourdequin (2019).
[147] Whyte (2012); Hourdequin (2019)   [148] Whyte (2018)   [149] Whyte (2018)
[150] Whyte (2012)   [151] Carr and Preston (2018)   [152] McLaren (2018)

Overall, these emerging understandings of what justice requires in the SG context can be understood as **geoengineering justice**, which demands a just approach to research and governance of SG.[153] Though all agree that justice issues and concerns are important for SG, experts also agree that fulfilling these demands for justice would be immensely challenging. There is much debate over to what extent and in what ways these demands could be met, and whether justice requires that SG research is enabled or restricted particularly in light of the many ethical challenges associated with SG that are discussed next. An illustration of many of the ideas discussed already can be found in Figure 11.

8.5 Ethical Concerns Associated with Solar Geoengineering

In addition to the previously mentioned ethical challenges directly related to justice, many other ethical challenges and concerns surrounding SG have been identified and explored. Most prominently, the **moral hazard** concern highlights the risk that attention toward SG could divert attention away from mitigation and adaptation, and that this diversion of attention away from more desirable climate responses would be morally problematic.[154] A related concern is that attention toward SG could be a manifestation of **moral corruption**, whereby particularly rich generations rationalize their own failure to address the ethical challenges posed by climate change in ways that are self-deceptive and self-serving.[155] The concern is that the rich may be tempted to shirk their moral responsibility to climate change in favor of inadequate solutions that serve their own more immediate ends.[156]

A related concern with moral implications is that SG may be embraced as a **technological fix**, or as an engineering solution for a social problem, sidestepping the need for massive social and behavioral change to address the root causes of climate change.[157] Ethical concerns are also raised by the possibility that attention toward SG creates **technological lock-in**, where the time and money invested in research incentivizes invested actors to push for a deployment, though it may violate procedural or distributive justice.[158] A deployment could mean that the options available to future generations are restricted in problematic ways, because they may need to maintain deployment to avoid termination shock (Section 6).[159]

Others suggest that the very idea of SG, as intentional climate change, is not ethically acceptable because it upends the proper relationship between humans and nonhuman species and the rest of nature.[160] Some argue the idea

---

[153] Hourdequin (2019)   [154] Lin (2013); Gardiner (2010)   [155] Gardiner (2010)
[156] Gardiner (2010)   [157] Weinberg (1966); Scott (2012)   [158] Hourdequin (2012)
[159] McKinnon (2019); Buck (2012)   [160] Hamilton (2013); Gardiner (2010)

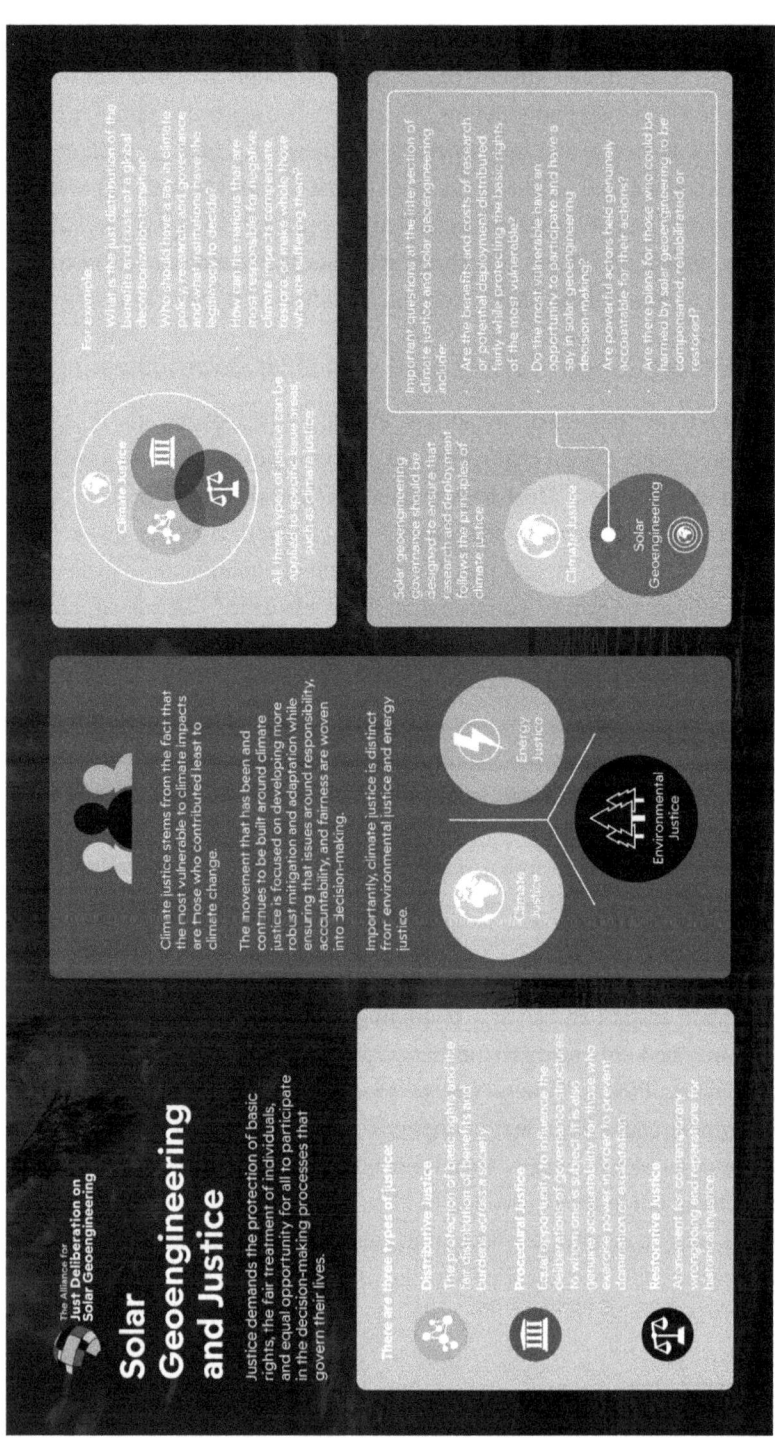

Figure 11 An illustration of the relationship between solar geoengineering and justice. A larger version of the figure is avaialble to view online at www.cambridge.org/jinnah-et-al

Source: The Alliance for Just Deliberation on Solar Geoengineering.

demonstrates human **hubris**, emblematic of arrogant tendencies to attempt to control nature to serve human interests.[161] Some argue that the Earth's natural systems, such as how sunlight enters the atmosphere, have a moral significance in itself, and intervening in these systems would be unethical without a strong justification.[162] Of course, the potential for harmful impacts on nonhuman species and ecosystems also raises ethical concerns.

A similar concern is that SG could exacerbate or lead to new forms of **domination**, which occurs when one individual or group can exercise superior power over another individual or group.[163] SG research could exacerbate international domination, for example, if it gives only rich countries the ability to deploy SG.[164] Such a situation would only deepen the power that rich countries have over poor countries, causing concern about the current highly unequal distribution of capabilities to research, deploy, and make or influence decisions about SG. Despite the need for just and participatory global research and decision-making, many agree that creating just global procedures faces many barriers, and it would be challenging, if not impossible, to secure agreement, consent, or consensus from everyone on decisions about whether and how to research and deploy SG. This is perhaps the biggest ethical challenge SG faces. Some are concerned that these tricky procedural questions would be sidestepped as climate change is increasingly perceived as an emergency that requires urgent responses.[165]

8.6 Reactions to Ethical Concerns

Experts have had two general reactions to the myriad ethical challenges described earlier. One reaction is to reject any further consideration of research or deployment of SG and instead advocate for restrictive forms of governance that would prohibit its use and most forms of research (Section 7).[166] The other general reaction is to attempt to determine what would make SG research or deployment ethically acceptable and to create principles that can guide the behavior of researchers, funders, decision-makers, and others to help ensure that research of SG only moves forward in ways that are ethical and just.

Whereas all ethicists agree that SG has serious ethical problems, some argue we need to approach climate justice by considering what justice requires given that the world has failed to mitigate climate change by reducing their emissions.[167] Under this approach, SG might be just if it compares favorably

---

[161] Jamieson (1996)   [162] Preston (2011)   [163] Smith (2018)   [164] Smith (2018)
[165] Preston (2013)
[166] Biermann et al. (2022); Gupta et al. (2024). For a response to Biermann et al. (2022), see Parson et al. (2024) and Weiners et al. (2023).
[167] Morrow and Svoboda (2016); Svoboda (2017)

to other available climate response options, none of which seem capable of safely restoring the climate by themselves in a world where we have failed to reduce emissions. In such a world, these ethicists argue that all courses of action carry ethical problems, and we are faced with comparing multiple imperfect options.[168]

Other experts question the idea we must choose between the **lesser of two evils**, or between a geoengineered world and a world where climate change is rampant.[169] This is because, as argued, there may be additional options that could be considered to avoid severe climate impacts but that are not politically palatable, and the uncertainty of SG's impacts mean we do not actually know whether it is less evil or harmful.[170]

The challenges and possibilities related to ethics and justice will continue to be a central part of discussions relating to whether and how SG research moves forward and how it could be governed. Emerging visions of geoengineering justice are beginning to identify what justice requires in the SG issue area. Nevertheless, even when concern for justice and the well-being of people and the planet is shared, there is disagreement over whether pursuing SG research is just or not. Like other aspects of SG, the ethics of SG are complicated and uncertain. As a minimum, a far more inclusive and meaningful discussion with publics and communities across the world on these critical issues is needed.

---

[168] Svoboda (2017)   [169] Gardiner (2010)   [170] Gardiner (2010); Whyte (2012)

References

American Geophysical Union. (2024). Ethical Framework Principles for Climate Intervention Research. *ESS Open Archive*. https://doi.org/10.22541/essoar.172917365.53105072/v1.

Bal, P. K., Pathak, R., Mishra, S. K., & Sahany, S. (2019). Effects of global warming and solar geoengineering on precipitation seasonality. *Environmental Research Letters*, *14*(3), 1–10. https://doi.org/10.1088/1748-9326/aafc7d.

Ballester, J., Quijal-Zamorano, M., Méndez Turrubiates, R.F., Pegenaute, F., Herrmann, F.R., Robine, J.M., Basagaña, X., Tonne, C., Antó, J.M., Achebak, H. (2023). Heat-related mortality in Europe during the summer of 2022. Nat Med 29, 1857–1866 . https://doi.org/10.1038/s41591-023-02419-z.

Barlevy, D., Juengst, E., Kahn, J. et al. (2024). Governing with public engagement: An anticipatory approach to human genome editing. *Science and Public Policy*, *51*(4), 680–691. https://doi.org/10.1093/scipol/scae010.

Baum, C. M., Fritz, L., Low, S., & Sovacool, B. K. (2024). Public perceptions and support of climate intervention technologies across the Global North and Global South. *Nature Communications*, *15*(1), 1–15. https://doi.org/10.1038/s41467-024-46341-5.

Bellamy, R., Chilvers, J., Vaughan, N. E., & Lenton, T. M. (2012). A review of climate geoengineering appraisals. *WIREs Climate Change*, *3*(6), 597–615. https://doi.org/10.1002/wcc.197.

Bhowmick, M., Mishra, S. K., Kravitz, B., Sahany, S., & Salunke, P. (2021). Response of the Indian summer monsoon to global warming, solar geoengineering and its termination. *Scientific Reports*, *11*(1), 1–11. https://doi.org/10.1038/s41598-021-89249-6.

Biber, E., & Ruhl, J. B. (2014). The permit power revisited: The theory and practice of regulatory permits in the administrative state. *Duke Law Journal*, *64*(2), 133–234.

Biermann, F., Oomen, J., Gupta, A. et al. (2022). Solar geoengineering: The case for an international non-use agreement. *Wiley Interdisciplinary Reviews: Climate Change*, *13*(3), 1–8.

Bishop, G. F., Oldendick, R. W., Tuchfarber, A. J., & Bennett, S. E. (1980). Pseudo-opinions on Public Affairs. *Public Opinion Quarterly*, *44*(2), 198–209. https://doi.org/10.1086/268584.

Bradburn, N. M., Sudman, S., & Wansink, B. (2004). *Asking Questions: The Definitive Guide to Questionnaire Design – For Market Research, Political Polls, and Social and Health Questionnaires* (2nd, Revised ed.). Jossey-Bass.

Buck, H. (2012). Climate remediation to address social development challenges: Going beyond cost-benefit and risk approaches to assessing solar radiation management. In *Engineering the Climate: The Ethics of Solar Radiation Management*. CJ Preston (ed.), Lexington Books.

Buck, H. J. (2022). Environmental Peacebuilding and Solar Geoengineering. *Frontiers in Climate*, 4. https://doi.org/10.3389/fclim.2022.869774.

Buck, H. J., Martin, L. J., Geden, O. et al. (2020). Evaluating the efficacy and equity of environmental stopgap measures. *Nature Sustainability*, 3(7), 499–504. https://doi.org/10.1038/s41893-020-0497-6.

Buck, H. J., Shah, P., Yang, J. Z., & Arpan, L. (2025). Public concerns about solar geoengineering research in the United States. *Communications Earth & Environment*, 6(1), 1–29. https://doi.org/10.1038/s43247-025-02595-5.

Burns, E. T., Flegal, J. A., Keith, D. W. et al. (2016). What do people think when they think about solar geoengineering? A review of empirical social science literature, and prospects for future research. *Earth's Future*, 4(11), 536–542. https://doi.org/10.1002/2016EF000461.

Burns, W., & Talati, S. (2025). *Updated report – The Solar Geoengineering Ecosystem: Key Actors Across the Landscape of the Field*. The Alliance for Just Deliberation on Solar Geoengineering (DSG) and the Forum on Climate Engineering Assessment (FCEA). https://sgdeliberation.org/publications/updated-solar-geoengineering-ecosystem/.

Busch, F., Krupa, J., & Harding, A. (2025). An Indigenous perspective on climate engineering. *Energy Research & Social Science*, 125,1–6. https://doi.org/10.1016/j.erss.2025.104117.

Cairns, R. C. (2014). Climate geoengineering: Issues of path-dependence and socio-technical lock-in. *WIREs Climate Change*, 5(5), 649–661. https://doi.org/10.1002/wcc.296.

Callies, D. E. (2019). The slippery slope argument against geoengineering research. *Journal of Applied Philosophy*, 36(4), 675–687. https://doi.org/10.1111/japp.12345.

Calvin, K., Dasgupta, D., Krinner, G. et al. 2023. "IPCC, 2023: Climate Change 2023: Synthesis Report. Contribution of Working Groups I, II and III to the Sixth Assessment Report of the Intergovernmental Panel on Climate Change [Core Writing Team, H. Lee and J. Romero (eds.)]. IPCC, Geneva, Switzerland." First. Intergovernmental Panel on Climate Change (IPCC). https://doi.org/10.59327/IPCC/AR6-9789291691647.

Caney, S. (2005). Cosmopolitan justice, responsibility, and global climate change. *Leiden Journal of International Law*, 18(4), 747–775. https://doi.org/10.1017/S0922156505002992.

Cao, L., & Jiang, J. (2017). Simulated effect of carbon cycle feedback on climate response to solar geoengineering. *Geophysical Research Letters*, *44*(24), 12,484–12,491. https://doi.org/10.1002/2017GL076546.

Carlisle, D. P., Feetham, P. M., Wright, M. J., & Teagle, D. A. H. (2020). The public remain uninformed and wary of climate engineering. *Climatic Change*, *160*(2), 303–322. https://doi.org/10.1007/s10584-020-02706-5.

Carlson, C. J., Colwell, R., Hossain, M. S. et al. (2022). Solar geoengineering could redistribute malaria risk in developing countries. *Nature Communications*, *13*(1), 1–9. https://doi.org/10.1038/s41467-022-29613-w.

Carr, W., & Preston, C. (2018). Recognitional justice, Climate Engineering, and the care approach. *Ethics, Policy & Environment*, *21*(*3*), 308–323.

Carr, W. A., Preston, C. J., Yung, L. et al. (2013). Public engagement on solar radiation management and why it needs to happen now. *Climatic Change*, *121*(3), 567–577. https://doi.org/10.1007/s10584-013-0763-y.

Casado Asensio, J., D. Blaquier, & J. Sedemund (2022), "Strengthening capacity for climate action in developing countries: Overview and recommendations," *OECD Development Co-operation Working Papers*, No. 106, OECD Publishing, Paris, https://doi.org/10.1787/0481c16a-en.

Cao, L., Jiang, J. (2017). Simulated Effect of Carbon Cycle Feedback on Climate Response to Solar Geoengineering. Geophysical Research Letters 44, 12,484-12,491. https://doi.org/10.1002/2017GL076546.

Checchi, F., Testa, A., Gimma, A., Koum-Besson, E., & Warsame, A. (2022). A method for small-area estimation of population mortality in settings affected by crises. *Population Health Metrics*, *20*(1), 4, 1–27. https://doi.org/10.1186/s12963-022-00283-6.

Chhetri, N., Chong, D., Conca, K. et al. (2018). *Governing solar radiation management*. Washington, DC: Forum for Climate Engineering Assessment, American University. https://doi.org/10.17606/M6SM17.

Clayton, S. (2020). Climate anxiety: Psychological responses to climate change. Journal of Anxiety Disorders 74, 102263. https://doi.org/10.1016/j.janxdis.2020.102263.

Condie, S. A., Anthony, K. R. N., Babcock, R. C. et al. (2021). Large-scale interventions may delay decline of the Great Barrier Reef. *Royal Society Open Science*, *8*(4),1–27. https://doi.org/10.1098/rsos.201296.

Craik, A. N., & Burns, W. C. G. (2016). *Climate Engineering under the Paris Agreement: A Legal and Policy Primer*. Centre for International Governance Innovation. www.cigionline.org/sites/default/files/documents/GeoEngineering%20Primer%20-%20Special%20Report.pdf.

Craik, A. N., & Moore, N. (2014). *Disclosure-Based Governance for Climate Engineering Research* (SSRN Scholarly Paper 2617339). https://papers.ssrn .com/abstract=2617339.

d'Angelo, C., Deshpande, A., Gloinson, E. R. et al. (2021). The Use of Public Engagement for Technological Innovation: Literature Review and Case Studies. *Gov.Uk Website (2021)*. www.rand.org/pubs/external_publications/ EP68481.html.

Dalby, S. (2015). Geoengineering: The next era of geopolitics? *Geography Compass*, *9*(4), 190–201. https://doi.org/10.1111/gec3.12195.

Directorate-General for Research and Innovation (European Commission) & Group of Chief Scientific Advisors (European Commission). (2024). *Solar radiation modification*. Publications Office of the European Union. https:// data.europa.eu/doi/10.2777/391614.

Dove, Z., Jinnah, S., & Talati, S. (2024a). Building capacity to govern emerging climate intervention technologies. *Elementa: Science of the Anthropocene*, *12*(1), 1–22. https://doi.org/10.1525/elementa.2023.00124.

Dove, Z., Hernandez, A., Talati, S., & Jinnah, S. (2024b). Global perspectives on solar geoengineering: A novel framework for analyzing research in pursuit of effective, inclusive, and just governance. *Energy Research & Social Science*, *118*, 1–18. https://doi.org/10.1016/j.erss.2024.103779.

Downs, A. (1957). *An Economic Theory of Democracy* (1st Ed). Harper and Row.

Dryzek, J. S., Nicol, D., Niemeyer, S. et al. (2020). Global citizen deliberation on genome editing. *Science*, *369*(6510), 1435–1437. https://doi.org/10.1126/ science.abb5931

Dyson, F. (1981). *Disturbing The Universe* (Sloan Foundation Science Series edition). Basic Books.

Eade, D. (2007). Capacity building: Who builds whose capacity? *Development in Practice*, *17*(4–5), 630–639. https://doi.org/10.1080/09614520701469807.

Eastham, S.D. (2015). Human health impacts of high altitude emissions (Thesis). Massachusetts Institute of Technology.

Eastham, S. D., Weisenstein, D. K., Keith, D. W., & Barrett, S. R. H. (2018). Quantifying the impact of sulfate geoengineering on mortality from air quality and UV-B exposure. *Atmospheric Environment*, *187*, 424–434. https://doi.org/10.1016/j.atmosenv.2018.05.047.

Edwards, M. (ed.) (2011). The Oxford Handbook of Civil Society, Oxford Handbooks (2011; online edn, Oxford Academic, 1 May 2012), https://doi .org/10.1093/oxfordhb/9780195398571.001.0001

Edwards, M. (ed.). (2013). *The Oxford Handbook of Civil Society* (Reprint edition). Oxford University Press.

Eitelwein, O., Fricker, R., Green, A., & Racloz, V. (2024). Quantifying the Impact of Climate Change on Human Health (Insight Report). World Economic Forum. www3.weforum.org/docs/WEF_Quantifying_the_ Impact_of_Climate_Change_on_Human_Health_2024.pdf.

European Commission: Directorate-General for Research and Innovation. (2002). Science and society : action plan. Publications Office of the European Union.

Farooque, M., & Kessler, J. L. (2023, January 9). How Would You Defend the Planet From Asteroids? *Issues in Science and Technology*. https://issues.org/ nasa-asteroid-initative-pta-farooque-kessler/.

Fiorino, D. J. (1990). Citizen participation and environmental risk: A survey of institutional mechanisms. *Science, Technology, & Human Values, 15*(2), 226–243. https://doi.org/10.1177/016224399001500204.

Fishkin, J. (2009). When the people speak: Deliberative democracy and public consultation. Oup Oxford.

Fishkin, J. S. (2011). *When the People Speak: Deliberative Democracy and Public Consultation* (Reprint edition). Oxford University Press.

Fishkin, J. S., Roy William Mayega, Lynn Atuyambe, Nathan Tumuhamye, Julius Ssentongo, Alice Siu, William Bazeyo (2017). Applying Deliberative Democracy in Africa: Uganda's First Deliberative Polls. Daedalus 2017; 146 (3): 140–154. doi: https://doi.org/10.1162/DAED_a_00453

Fishkin, J., Siu, A., Diamond, L., & Bradburn, N. (2021). Is deliberation an antidote to extreme partisan polarization? Reflections on "America in One Room." *American Political Science Review, 115*(4), 1464–1481. https://doi .org/10.1017/S0003055421000642.

Flavelle, C., & Bates, I. C. (2024, April 2). Warming Is Getting Worse. So They Just Tested a Way to Deflect the Sun. *The New York Times*. www.nytimes .com/2024/04/02/climate/global-warming-clouds-solar-geoengineering.html.

Flegal, J. A., Hubert, A.-M., Morrow, D. R., & Moreno-Cruz, J. B. (2019). Solar geoengineering: Social science, legal, ethical, and economic frameworks. *Annual Review of Environment and Resources, 44*, 399–423. https://doi.org/ 10.1146/annurev-environ-102017-030032.

Florini, A., & Sovacool, B. K. (2009). Who governs energy? The challenges facing global energy governance. *Energy Policy, 37*(12), 5239–5248. https:// doi.org/10.1016/j.enpol.2009.07.039.

Forsyth, M., Cleland, D., Tepper, F., Hollingworth, D., Soares, M., Nairn, A., Wilkinson, C., (2021). A future agenda for environmental restorative justice? The International Journal of Restorative Justice 4, 17–40. https://doi.org/ 10.5553/TIJRJ.000063

Fraser, N., & Honneth, A. (2003). *Redistribution or Recognition?: A Political-Philosophical Exchange*. Verso.

Fritz, L., Baum, C. M., Low, S., & Sovacool, B. K. (2024). Public engagement for inclusive and sustainable governance of climate interventions. *Nature Communications, 15*(1), 1–17. https://doi.org/10.1038/s41467-024-48510-y.

Funtowicz, S. O., & Ravetz, J. R. (1993). Science for the post-normal age. *Futures, 25*(7), 739–755. https://doi.org/10.1016/0016-3287(93)90022-L.

Gardiner, S. (2010). Is 'arming the future' with geoengineering really the lesser evil? Some doubts about the ethics of intentionally manipulating the climate system. *Climate Ethics: Essential Readings, Oxford.* https://papers.ssrn.com/sol3/papers.cfm?abstract_id=1357162

Gardiner, S. M. (2014). A call for a global constitutional convention focused on future generations. *Ethics & International Affairs, 28*(3), 299–315. https://doi.org/10.1017/S0892679414000379.

Gardiner, S. M., & Fragnière, A. (2018). The tollgate principles for the governance of geoengineering: Moving beyond the Oxford principles to an ethically more robust approach. *Ethics, Policy & Environment, 21*(2), 143–174. https://doi.org/10.1080/21550085.2018.1509472.

Gottfried, J. (2024, January 31). Americans' Social Media Use. *Pew Research Center.* www.pewresearch.org/internet/2024/01/31/americans-social-media-use/

Gordon, D.J., Johnson, C.A., (2018). City-networks, global climate governance, and the road to 1.5°C. Current Opinion in Environmental Sustainability, 1.5°C Climate change and urban areas 30, 35–41. https://doi.org/10.1016/j.cosust.2018.02.011

Government Accountability Office (GAO) (2016). *Open Innovation: Practices to Engage Citizens and Effectively Implement Federal Initiatives.* Report to Congressional Committees, October.

Grant, N., Robock, A., Xia, L., Singh, J., & Clark, B. (2025). Impacts on Indian agriculture due to stratospheric aerosol intervention using agroclimatic indices. *Earth's Future, 13*(1), 1–17. https://doi.org/10.1029/2024EF005262.

Grossi, G., Goglio, P., Vitali, A., & Williams, A. G. (2019). Livestock and climate change: Impact of livestock on climate and mitigation strategies. *Animal Frontiers, 9*(1), 69–76. https://doi.org/10.1093/af/vfy034.

Grubert, E. (2024). *Societal Considerations, Impacts, and Public Engagement for Atmospheric Methane Removal Technologies,* Commissed Paper for the National Academies of Science, Engineering and Medicine Committee. Available at: https://nap.nationalacademies.org/resource/27157/grubert-com misionedpaper.pdf Accessed 29 November 2025.

Grunwald, A. (2018). *Technology Assessment in Practice and Theory.* Routledge. https://doi.org/10.4324/9780429442643.

Gupta, A., Biermann, F., Driel, E. van et al. (2024). Towards a non-use regime on solar geoengineering: Lessons from international law and governance.

Transnational Environmental Law, *13*(2), 368–399. https://doi.org/10.1017/S2047102524000050.

Gupta, A., Möller, I., Biermann, F. et al. (2020). Anticipatory governance of solar geoengineering: Conflicting visions of the future and their links to governance proposals. *Current Opinion in Environmental Sustainability*, *45*, 10–19. https://doi.org/10.1016/j.cosust.2020.06.004.

Guston, D. H. (2014). Understanding "'anticipatory governance." *Social Studies of Science*, *44*(2), 218–242. https://doi.org/10.1177/0306312713508669.

Guston, D. H. (2023). *Governing Science, Technology, and Innovation in Hotter Times*, 1–9. https://doi.org/10.7551/mitpress/15122.003.0011.

Hale, T.N., Chan, S., Hsu, A., Clapper, A., Elliott, C., Faria, P., Kuramochi, T., McDaniel, S., Morgado, M., Roelfsema, M., Santaella, M., Singh, N., Tout, I., Weber, C., Weinfurter, A., Widerberg, O., (2021). Sub- and non-state climate action: a framework to assess progress, implementation and impact. Climate Policy 21, 406–420. https://doi.org/10.1080/14693062.2020.1828796.

Hamilton, C. (2013). *Earthmasters: The Dawn of the Age of Climate Engineering*. Yale University Press.

Hansen, J.E., Sato, M., Simons, L., Nazarenko, L.S., Sangha, I., Kharecha, P., Zachos, J.C., von Schuckmann, K., Loeb, N.G., Osman, M.B., Jin, Q., Tselioudis, G., Jeong, E., Lacis, A., Ruedy, R., Russell, G., Cao, J., Li, J., (2023). Global warming in the pipeline. Oxford Open Climate Change 3, kgad008. https://doi.org/10.1093/oxfclm/kgad008.

Harding, A., Vecchi, G. A., Yang, W., & Keith, D. W. (2024). Impact of solar geoengineering on temperature-attributable mortality. *Proceedings of the National Academy of Sciences*, *121*(52),1–9. https://doi.org/10.1073/pnas.2401801121.

Hassan, A. (2024, March 19). A Controversial SRM Resolution Was Withdrawn at UNEA-6: Here's our Takeaway. *The Alliance for Just Deliberation on Solar Geoengineering*. https://sgdeliberation.org/a-controversial-srm-resolution-was-withdrawn-at-unea-6-heres-our-takeaway/.

Horton, J., & Keith, D. (2016). Solar geoengineering and obligations to the global poor. In J. Preston (Ed.), *Climate Justice and Geoengineering: Ethics and Policy in the Atmospheric Anthropocene*, Rowman & Littlefield, 79–92.

Horton, J. B., Smith, W., & Keith, D. W. (2025). Who could deploy stratospheric aerosol injection? The United States, China, and large-scale, Rapid Planetary Cooling. *Global Policy* 16: 514–524. https://doi.org/10.1111/1758-5899.70015.

Hourdequin, M. (2012). Geoengineering, solidarity, and moral risk. In Preston J. C. (ed.) *Engineering the Climate: The Ethics of Solar Radiation Management*, Bloomsbury Publishing PLC, pp. 15–32.

Hourdequin, M. (2019). Geoengineering justice: The role of recognition. *Science, Technology, & Human Values*, *44*(3), 448–477. https://doi.org/10.1177/0162243918802893.

Hubert, A.-M. (2021). A code of conduct for responsible geoengineering research. *Global Policy*, *12*(S1), 82–96. https://doi.org/10.1111/1758-5899.12845.

Hutchins, J. A. (2020). Tailoring scientific communications for audience and research narrative. *Current Protocols Essential Laboratory Techniques*, *20*(1), 1–13. https://doi.org/10.1002/cpet.40.

IPCC. (2014). "Climate Change 2014: Synthesis Report. Contribution of Working Groups I, II and III to the Fifth Assessment Report of the Intergovernmental Panel on Climate Change," Core Writing Team, R. K. Pachauri and L. A. Meyer (eds.). IPCC, Geneva, Switzerland, p. 151.

IPCC. (2022). "Climate Change 2022: Impacts, Adaptation and Vulnerability. Contribution of Working Group II to the Sixth Assessment Report of the Intergovernmental Panel on Climate Change." H.-O. Pörtner, D. C. Roberts, M. Tignor et al. (eds.). Cambridge University Press, Cambridge and New York, pp. 2411–2538, https://doi.org/10.1017/9781009325844.025.

Irvine, P., Emanuel, K., He, J. et al. (2019). Halving warming with idealized solar geoengineering moderates key climate hazards. *Nature Climate Change*, *9*(4), 295–299. https://doi.org/10.1038/s41558-019-0398-8.

Irvine, P. J., Kravitz, B., Lawrence, M. G. et al. (2017). Towards a comprehensive climate impacts assessment of solar geoengineering. *Earth's Future*, *5*(1), 93–106. https://doi.org/10.1002/2016EF000389.

Irvine, P. J., Kravitz, B., Lawrence, M. G., & Muri, H. (2016). An overview of the Earth system science of solar geoengineering. *WIREs Climate Change*, *7*(6), 815–833. https://doi.org/10.1002/wcc.423.

Jackson, L. S., Crook, J. A., Jarvis, A. et al. (2015). Assessing the controllability of Arctic sea ice extent by sulfate aerosol geoengineering. *Geophysical Research Letters*, *42*(4), 1223–1231. https://doi.org/10.1002/2014GL062240.

Jamieson, D. (1996). Ethics and intentional climate change. *Climatic Change*, *33*(3), 323–336. https://doi.org/10.1007/BF00142580.

Janssens, M., de Vries, I. E., Hulshoff, S. J., & DSE 16-02. (2020). A specialised delivery system for stratospheric sulphate aerosols: Design and operation. *Climatic Change*, *162*(1), 67–85. https://doi.org/10.1007/s10584-020-02740-3.

Jinnah, Sikina. (2018) "Why Govern Climate Engineering? A Preliminary Framework for Demand-Based Governance. *International Studies Review*. 20(2), 272–282.

Jinnah, S., Bedsworth, L., Talati, S. et al. (2024). Final Report of the SCoPEx Advisory Committee. March 18. SCoPEX Advisory Committee. https://salatainstitute.harvard.edu/an-update-on-scopex/.

Jinnah, S., & Nicholson, S. (2019). The hidden politics of climate engineering. *Nature Geoscience*, *12*(11), 876–879. https://doi.org/10.1038/s41561-019-0483-7.

Jinnah, S., Talati, S., Bedsworth, L. et al. (2024a). Do small outdoor geoengineering experiments require governance? *Science*, *385*(6709), 600–603. https://doi.org/10.1126/science.adn2853.

Jones, A., Haywood, J., & Boucher, O. (2009). Climate impacts of geoengineering marine stratocumulus clouds. *Journal of Geophysical Research: Atmospheres*, *114*(D10), 1–9. https://doi.org/10.1029/2008JD011450.

Joss, S. and Bellucci, S. (ed.) (2002). *Participatory technology assessment: European perspectives*. London: Centre for Study of Democracy, University of Westminster.

Kaplan, L., John N., David T., Mahmud F., Jason L., Mark N., Bjørn B., & Dan S. "Cooling a Warming Planet? Public Forums on Climate Intervention Research." Washington, DC: ASU Consortium for Science, Policy & Outcomes (November 2019).

Kaplan, L. R., Farooque, M., Sarewitz, D., & Tomblin, D. (2021). Designing participatory technology assessments: A reflexive method for advancing the public role in science policy decision-making. *Technological Forecasting and Social Change*, *171*, 1–9. https://doi.org/10.1016/j.techfore.2021.120974.

Keith, D. W., & Irvine, P. J. (2016). Solar geoengineering could substantially reduce climate risks – A research hypothesis for the next decade. *Earth's Future*, *4*(11), 549–559. https://doi.org/10.1002/2016EF000465.

Khan, M. R., Roberts, J. T., Huq, S., & Hoffmeister, V. (2018). *The Paris framework for climate change capacity building*. Routledge.

Kubin, E., & von Sikorski, C. (2021). The role of (social) media in political polarization: A systematic review. *Annals of the International Communication Association*, *45*(3), 188–206. https://doi.org/10.1080/23808985.2021.1976070.

Lauvset, S. K., Tjiputra, J., & Muri, H. (2017). Climate engineering and the ocean: Effects on biogeochemistry and primary production. *Biogeosciences*, *14*(24), 5675–5691. https://doi.org/10.5194/bg-14-5675-2017.

Lavery, J. V. (2018). Building an evidence base for stakeholder engagement. *Science*, *361*(6402), 554–556. https://doi.org/10.1126/science.aat8429.

Least Developed Countries (LDC) Initiative for Effective Adaptation and Resilience's. (2019). *LDC 2050: Toward a climate-resilient future*. LDC Initiative for Effective Adaptation and Resilience. www.ldc-climate.org/wp-content/uploads/2019/09/2050-Vision.pdf. Accessed May 24, 2024.

Lewandowsky, S., & van der Linden, S. (2021). Countering misinformation and fake news through inoculation and prebunking. *European Review of Social*

Psychology, 32(2), 348–384. https://doi.org/10.1080/10463283.2021 .1876983.

Lin, A. C. (2013). Does geoengineering present a moral hazard. *Ecology Law Quarterly, 40*, 693–688.

Lin, A. C. (2020). Avoiding lock-in of solar geoengineering. *Northern Kentucky Law Review, 47*, 139–154.

Long, J. C. S., & Shepherd, J. G. (2014). The strategic value of Geoengineering Research. In B. Freedman (ed.), *Global Environmental Change* (pp. 757–770). Springer. https://doi.org/10.1007/978-94-007-5784-4_24.

Loucks, D. P. (2021). Chapter 2 – Impacts of climate change on economies, ecosystems, energy, environments, and human equity: A systems perspective. In T. M. Letcher (ed.), *The Impacts of Climate Change* (pp. 19–50). Elsevier. https://doi.org/10.1016/B978-0-12-822373-4.00016-1.

Low, S., Baum, C. M., & Sovacool, B. K. (2022). Taking it outside: Exploring social opposition to 21 early-stage experiments in radical climate interventions. *Energy Research & Social Science, 90*, 102594, 1–21. https://doi.org/ 10.1016/j.erss.2022.102594.

MacMartin, D. G., Kravitz, B., Long, J. C. S., & Rasch, P. J. (2016). Geoengineering with stratospheric aerosols: What do we not know after a decade of research? *Earth's Future, 4*(11), 543–548. https://doi.org/10.1002/ 2016EF000418.

MacMartin, D. G., Ricke, K. L., & Keith, D. W. (2018). Solar geoengineering as part of an overall strategy for meeting the 1.5°C Paris target. *Philosophical Transactions of the Royal Society A: Mathematical, Physical and Engineering Sciences, 376*(2119), 20160454, 1–19. https://doi.org/10.1098/ rsta.2016.0454.

Macnaghten, P., & Owen, R. (2011). Good governance for geoengineering. *Nature, 479*(7373), 293–293. https://doi.org/10.1038/479293a.

Mansbridge, J. (2010). Deliberative polling as the gold standard. *The Good Society, 19*(1), 55–62. https://doi.org/10.5325/goodsociety.19.1.0055.

McKinnon, C. (2011). *Climate Change and Future Justice: Precaution, Compensation and Triage*. Routledge. https://doi.org/10.4324/ 9780203802205.

McKinnon, C. (2019). Sleepwalking into lock-in? Avoiding wrongs to future people in the governance of solar radiation management research. *Environmental Politics, 28*(3), 441–459. https://doi.org/10.1080/ 09644016.2018.1450344.

McKinnon, C. (2022). Climate Change and Political Theory, 1st edition. ed. Polity, Cambridge, UK Hoboken, NJ, USA.

McLaren, D. P. (2018). In a broken world: Towards an ethics of repair in the Anthropocene. *The Anthropocene Review, 5*(2), 136–154. https://doi.org/10.1177/2053019618767211.

Morrow, D., & Svoboda, T. (2016). Geoengineering and non-ideal theory. *Public Affairs Quarterly, 30*(1), 83–102.

NASA. (2001, June 15). *Global Effects of Mount Pinatubo* [Text.Article]. NASA Earth Observatory. https://earthobservatory.nasa.gov/images/1510/global-effects-of-mount-pinatubo.

National Academies of Sciences, Engineering, and Medicine (NASEM). (2017). *Communicating Science Effectively: A Research Agenda*. National Academies Press. https://doi.org/10.17226/23674.

National Academies of Sciences, Engineering, and Medicine (NASEM). (2021). *Reflecting Sunlight: Recommendations for Solar Geoengineering Research and Research Governance*. Washington, DC: The National Academies Press. https://doi.org/10.17226/25762.

National Institutes of Health. N.d. Clear Communication Resource Pages. www.nih.gov/institutes-nih/nih-office-director/office-communications-pub lic-liaison/clear-communication.

Nelson, S. C. (2020). *Scientists Trial World-First "Cloud Brightening" Technique to Protect Corals*. www.scu.edu.au/news/2020/scientists-trial-world-first-cloud-brightening-technique-to-protect-corals.php.

O'Doherty, K., & Einsiedel, E. (2013). *Public Engagement and Emerging Technologies*. University of British Columbia Press.

Office of Management and Budget (OMB) (2021). *Study to Identify Methods to Assess Equity: Report to the President*. Practices to Engage Citizens and Effectively Implement Federal Initiatives, July.

Office, U. S. G. A. (2016, October 13). *Open Innovation: Practices to Engage Citizens and Effectively Implement Federal Initiatives | U.S. GAO*. www.gao .gov/products/gao-17-14.

Parker, A. (2014). Governing solar geoengineering research as it leaves the laboratory. *Philosophical Transactions of the Royal Society A: Mathematical, Physical and Engineering Sciences, 372*(2031), 20140173, 1–17. https://doi .org/10.1098/rsta.2014.0173.

Parkes, B., Challinor, A., & Nicklin, K. (2015). Crop failure rates in a geoengi-neered climate: Impact of climate change and marine cloud brightening. *Environmental Research Letters, 10*(8), 084003, 1–7. https://doi.org/10.1088/1748-9326/10/8/084003.

Parson, E. A., Buck, H. J., Jinnah, S., Moreno-Cruz, J., & Nicholson, S. (2024). Toward an evidence-informed, responsible, and inclusive debate on solar geoengineering: A response to the proposed non-use agreement. *WIREs Climate Change, 15*(5), 1–9. https://doi.org/10.1002/wcc.903.

Parson, E. A., & Keith, D. W. (2024). Solar geoengineering: History, methods, governance, prospects. *Annual Review of Environment and Resources, 49,* 337–366. https://doi.org/10.1146/annurev-environ-112321-081911.

Pellow, D. N. (2017). *What Is Critical Environmental Justice?* (1st ed.). Polity.

Pidgeon, N., Parkhill, K., Corner, A., & Vaughan, N. (2013). Deliberating stratospheric aerosols for climate geoengineering and the SPICE project. *Nature Climate Change, 3*(5), Article 5, 451–457. https://doi.org/10.1038/nclimate1807.

Pogrebinschi, T., & Ross, M. (2019). 26. Democratic innovations in Latin America. *Handbook of Democratic Innovation and Governance,* 389. Edward Elgar.

Potochnik, A., & Jacquart, M. (2025). *Public Engagement with Science: Defining the Project.* Cambridge University Press. https://doi.org/10.1017/9781009475105.

President's Council of Advisors on Science and Technology (PCAST) (2023). *Letter to the President: Advancing Public Engagement with the Sciences.*

Preston, C. J. (2011). Re-thinking the unthinkable: Environmental ethics and the presumptive argument against geoengineering. *Environmental Values, 20*(4), 457–479.

Preston, C. J. (2012). *Engineering the Climate: The Ethics of Solar Radiation Management.* Rowman & Littlefield.

Preston, C. J. (2013). Ethics and geoengineering: Reviewing the moral issues raised by solar radiation management and carbon dioxide removal. *WIREs Climate Change, 4*(1), 23–37. https://doi.org/10.1002/wcc.198.

Preston, C. J. (2016). *Climate justice and geoengineering: Ethics and policy in the atmospheric anthropocene.* Rowman & Littlefield. https://books.google.com/books?hl=en&lr=&id=UeLaDwAAQBAJ&oi=fnd&pg=PP1&dq=preston+climate+justice+and+geoengineering&ots=t6YlLwaEoY&sig=DBvhJOPqp01WgOHxR9RVcK4wZr8.

Prosser, C., & Mellon, J. (2018). The twilight of the polls? A review of trends in polling accuracy and the causes of polling misses. *Government and Opposition, 53*(4), 757–790. https://doi.org/10.1017/gov.2018.7.

Rayner, S., Heyward, C., Kruger, T. et al. (2013). The Oxford Principles. *Climatic Change, 121*(3), 499–512. https://doi.org/10.1007/s10584-012-0675-2.

Reidmiller, D. R., Avery, C. W., Easterling, D. R. et al. (n.d.). *Impacts, Risks, and Adaptation in the United States: Fourth National Climate Assessment, Volume II.* https://doi.org/10.7930/NCA4.2018.

Rerolle, F., Arnold, B. F., & Benmarhnia, T. (2023). Excess risk in infant mortality among populations living in flood-prone areas in Bangladesh: A cluster-matched cohort study over three decades, 1988 to 2017. *Proceedings of the National Academy of Sciences, 120*(50), e2218789120, 1–8. https://doi.org/10.1073/pnas.2218789120.

Reynolds, J. L., Contreras, J. L., & Sarnoff, J. D. (2017). Solar climate engineering and intellectual property: Toward a research commons. *Minnesota Journal of Law, Science and Technology, 18*(1), 1–110.

Richter, J., Bernstein, M. J., & Farooque, M. (2022). The process to find a process for governance: Nuclear waste management and consent-based siting in the United States. *Energy Research & Social Science, 87*, 102473. https://doi.org/10.1016/j.erss.2021.102473.

Ricke, K. L., Morgan, M. G., & Allen, M. R. (2010). Regional climate response to solar-radiation management. *Nature Geoscience, 3*(8), 537–541. https://doi.org/10.1038/ngeo915.

Ricke, K., Wan, J. S., Saenger, M., & Lutsko, N. J. (2023). Hydrological consequences of solar geoengineering. *Annual Review of Earth and Planetary Sciences, 51*, 447–470. https://doi.org/10.1146/annurev-earth-031920-083456.

Schlosberg, D. (2007). *Defining Environmental Justice: Theories, Movements, and Nature.* Oxford University Press. https://doi.org/10.1093/acprof:oso/9780199286294.001.0001.

Schlosberg, D., & Carruthers, D. (2010). Indigenous struggles, environmental justice, and community capabilities. *Global Environmental Politics, 10*(4), 12–35. https://doi.org/10.1162/GLEP_a_00029.

Schlosberg, D., & Collins, L. B. (2014). From environmental to climate justice: Climate change and the discourse of environmental justice. *WIREs Climate Change, 5*(3), 359–374. https://doi.org/10.1002/wcc.275.

Sclove, R. (2010). *Reinventing Technology Assessment: A 21st Century Model.* Woodrow Wilson International Center for Scholars.

Scott, D. (2012). Insurance policy or technological fix: The ethical implications of framing solar radiation management. In: Preston, C, ed. *Engineering the Climate: The Ethics of Solar Radiation Management*, Lanham, MD: Lexington Press; 2012, 113–131.

Scott-Buechler, C., & Jinnah, S. (2024). Early engagement will be necessary for atmospheric methane removal field trials. *Environmental Research Letters, 19*(11), 111010, 1–7. https://doi.org/10.1088/1748-9326/ad7c69.

Sen, A. (2011). *The Idea of Justice* (Reprint edition). Belknap Press.

Shepherd, J., Caldeira, K., Cox, P. et al. (2009). *Geoengineering the climate*: Science, governance and uncertainty (pp. 1–98). The Royal Society.

Shue, H. (2024). *The Pivotal Generation: Why We Have a Moral Responsibility to Slow Climate Change Right Now.* Princeton University Press.

Sittenfeld, D., Farooque, M., Helmuth, B. et al. (2022). Citizen science, civics, and resilient communities: Informing community resilience policies through local knowledge, community values, and community-generated data. *Citizen Science: Theory and Practice, 7*(1), 1–18. https://doi.org/10.5334/cstp.516.

Smith, P. T. (2018). Legitimacy and non-domination in solar radiation management research. *Ethics, Policy & Environment, 21*(3), 341–361. https://doi.org/10.1080/21550085.2018.1562528.

Smith, W., & Wagner, G. (2018). Stratospheric aerosol injection tactics and costs in the first 15 years of deployment. *Environmental Research Letters, 13* (12), 1–12. https://doi.org/10.1088/1748-9326/aae98d.

Stanford Deliberative Democracy Lab. (1998, February 28). *Deliberative Polling®: Texas Electric Utilities | Deliberative Democracy Lab*. https://deliberation.stanford.edu/news/deliberative-pollingr-texas-electric-utilities.

Stanford Deliberative Democracy Lab. (2017a, April 29). *Mongolia's First National Deliberative Poll on Constitutional Amendments | Deliberative Democracy Lab*. https://deliberation.stanford.edu/news/mongolias-first-national-deliberative-poll-constitutional-amendments.

Stanford Deliberative Democracy Lab. (2017b, August 30). *Deliberation in South Korea on Closing Two Nuclear Reactors | Deliberative Democracy Lab*. https://deliberation.stanford.edu/news/deliberation-south-korea-closing-two-nuclear-reactors.

Stanford Deliberative Democracy Lab. (2023, June 22). *Results of First Global Deliberative Poll® Announced by Stanford's*. https://cddrl.fsi.stanford.edu/news/results-first-global-deliberative-pollr-announced-stanfords-deliberative-democracy-lab.

Stanford Deliberative Democracy Lab. (2024). *Deliberative Polling on Antibiotic Resistance | Deliberative Democracy Lab*. https://deliberation.stanford.edu/deliberative-polling-antibiotic-resistance.

Stilgoe, J. (2015). *Experiment Earth: Responsible Innovation in Geoengineering*. Routledge.

Stilgoe, J. (2016). Geoengineering as collective experimentation. *Science and Engineering Ethics, 22*(3), 851–869. https://doi.org/10.1007/s11948-015-9646-0.

Stilgoe, J., Owen, R., & Macnaghten, P. (2013a). Developing a framework for responsible innovation. *Research Policy, 42*(9), 1568–1580. https://doi.org/10.1016/j.respol.2013.05.008.

Stilgoe, J., Watson, M., & Kuo, K. (2013b). Public engagement with biotechnologies offers lessons for the governance of geoengineering research and beyond. *PLOS Biology, 11*(11), 1–7. https://doi.org/10.1371/journal.pbio.1001707.

Stirling, A. (2008). "Opening Up" and "Closing Down": Power, participation, and pluralism in the social appraisal of technology. *Science, Technology, & Human Values, 33*(2), 262–294. https://doi.org/10.1177/0162243907311265.

Sunstein, C. R. (2017). *#Republic: Divided Democracy in the Age of Social Media.* Princeton University Press.

Svoboda, T. (2017). *The Ethics of Climate Engineering: Solar Radiation Management and Non-Ideal Justice.* Taylor & Francis.

Svoboda, T., & Irvine, P. (2014). Ethical and technical challenges in compensating for harm due to solar radiation Management geoengineering. *Ethics, Policy & Environment, 17*(2), 157–174. https://doi.org/10.1080/21550085.2014.927962.

Svoboda, T., Keller, K., Goes, M., & Tuana, N. (2011). Sulfate aerosol geoengineering: The question of justice. *Public Affairs Quarterly, 25*(3), 157–179.

Táíwò, O. O., & Talati, S. (2021). Who are the engineers? Solar geoengineering research and justice. *Global Environmental Politics, 22*(1), 12–18. https://doi.org/10.1162/glep_a_00620.

Táíwò, O. O., & Talati, S. (2022). Who are the engineers? Solar geoengineering research and justice. *Global Environmental Politics, 22*(1), 12–18.

Tang, A. (2023). The slippery slopes of climate engineering research. *Global Environmental Change, 80,* 1–11. https://doi.org/10.1016/j.gloenvcha.2023.102674.

The Alliance for Just Deliberation on Solar Geoengineering (DSG) (2023). "Building Solar Geoengineering Governance Capacity." https://sgdelibera tion.org/wp-content/uploads/2023/04/DSG-White-Paper_Capacity-Building.pdf.

The Alliance for Just Deliberation on Solar Geoengineering (DSG). (2024). "Insights into Our Global Engagement Decision-Making: Where We Go and Why?" https://sgdeliberation.org/wp-content/uploads/2024/06/Insights-into-our-global-engagement-decision-making.pdf.

Tilmes, S., Fasullo, J., Lamarque, J.-F. et al. (2013). The hydrological impact of geoengineering in the Geoengineering Model Intercomparison Project (GeoMIP). *Journal of Geophysical Research: Atmospheres, 118*(19), 11,036–11,058. https://doi.org/10.1002/jgrd.50868.

Tilmes, S., Jahn, A., Kay, J. E., Holland, M., & Lamarque, J.-F. (2014). Can regional climate engineering save the summer Arctic sea ice? *Geophysical Research Letters, 41*(3), 880–885. https://doi.org/10.1002/2013GL058731.

Tilmes, S., Visioni, D., Jones, A. et al. (2022). Stratospheric ozone response to sulfate aerosol and solar dimming climate interventions based on the G6 Geoengineering Model Intercomparison Project (GeoMIP) simulations. *Atmospheric Chemistry and Physics, 22*(7), 4557–4579. https://doi.org/10.5194/acp-22-4557-2022.

Tomblin, D., Pirtle, Z., Farooque, M. et al. (2017). Integrating public deliberation into Engineering Systems: Participatory technology assessment of NASA's Asteroid Redirect Mission. *Astropolitics*, *15*(2), 141–166. https://doi.org/10.1080/14777622.2017.1340823.

Trisos, C. H., Gabriel, C., Robock, A., & Xia, L. (2018). Chapter 24 – Ecological, agricultural, and health impacts of solar geoengineering. In Z. Zommers & K. Alverson (eds.), *Resilience* (pp. 291–303). Elsevier. https://doi.org/10.1016/B978-0-12-811891-7.00024-4.

UN Atlas of the Oceans. (n.d.). *UN Atlas of the Oceans: Subtopic*. Retrieved February 12, 2025, from www.oceansatlas.org/subtopic/en/c/114/.

United Nations. (2025, January 10). *Confirmed: 2024 Was the Hottest Year on Record, Says UN Weather Agency | UN News*. https://news.un.org/en/story/2025/01/1158891.

United Nations Environment Programme (2023). *One Atmosphere: An Independent Expert Review on Solar Radiation Modification Research and Deployment*. https://wedocs.unep.org/20.500.11822/41903.

United Nations Human Rights Council Advisory Committee. (2023). "Impact of New Technologies for Climate Protection on the Enjoyment of Human Rights." A/HRC/54/47. Thematic Report. https://documents.un.org/doc/undoc/gen/g23/141/86/pdf/g2314186.pdf?token=Bno9GEzi2XEbimgqzO&fe=true, Accessed February 6, 2024.

USGCRP, 2018: Impacts, Risks, and Adaptation in the United States: Fourth National Climate Assessment, Volume II [Reidmiller, D.R., C.W. Avery, D. R. Easterling, K.E. Kunkel, K.L.M. Lewis, T.K. Maycock, and B.C. Stewart (eds.)]. U.S. Global Change Research Program, Washington, DC, USA, 1506 pp. doi: 10.7930/NCA4.2018.

Vicedo-Cabrera, A. M., Scovronick, N., Sera, F. et al. (2021). The burden of heat-related mortality attributable to recent human-induced climate change. *Nature Climate Change*, *11*(6), 492–500. https://doi.org/10.1038/s41558-021-01058-x.

Visioni, D., Slessarev, E., MacMartin, D. G. et al. (2020). What goes up must come down: Impacts of deposition in a sulfate geoengineering scenario. *Environmental Research Letters*, *15*(9), 1–8. https://doi.org/10.1088/1748-9326/ab94eb.

Weinberg, A. M. (1966). Can technology replace Social Engineering? *Bulletin of the Atomic Scientists*, *22*(10), 4–8. https://doi.org/10.1080/00963402.1966.11454993.

Weitzman, M. L. (2015). A voting architecture for the governance of free-driver externalities, with application to geoengineering. *The Scandinavian Journal of Economics*, *117*(4), 1049–1068. https://doi.org/10.1111/sjoe.12120.

Weller, N., Govani, M.S., & Farooque, M. (2025). "Supporting Federal Decision Making through Participatory Technology Assessment." *Day One Project*. https://fas.org/publication/supporting-federal-decision-making-through-participatory-technology-assessment/.

WHO, & UNICEF. (2023). *From insight to action: Examining mortality in Somalia*. www.unicef.org/esa/media/12316/file/From-Insight-to-Action-Somalia-2023.pdf.

Whyte, K.P., (2011). The Recognition Dimensions of Environmental Justice in Indian Country. Environmental Justice 4, 199–205. https://doi.org/10.1089/env.2011.0036.

Whyte, K. P. (2012). Now This! Indigenous sovereignty, political obliviousness and governance models for SRM research. *Ethics, Policy & Environment*, *15*(2), 172–187. https://doi.org/10.1080/21550085.2012.685570.

Whyte, K. P. (2018). Indigeneity in geoengineering discourses: Some considerations. *Ethics, Policy & Environment*, *21*(3), 289–307. https://doi.org/10.1080/21550085.2018.1562529.

Wieners, C. E., Hofbauer, B. P., de Vries, I. E. et al. (2023). Solar radiation modification is risky, but so is rejecting it: A call for balanced research. *Oxford Open Climate Change*, *3*(1), 1–4. https://doi.org/10.1093/oxfclm/kgad002.

Wilsdon, J., & Willis, R. (2004). *See-Through Science: Why Public Engagement Needs to Move Upstream*. Demos.

World Commission of UNESCO on the Ethics of Scientific Knowledge and Technology (COMEST). (2024). Report of the World Commission on the Ethics of Scientific Knowledge and Technology (COMEST) on the Ethics of Climate Engineering. SHS/COMEST-13/2023/1REV. https://unesdoc.unesco.org/ark:/48223/pf0000386677.locale=en.

Worthington, R., Cavalier, D., Farooque, M. et al. (2012a). *Technology Assessment and Public Participation: From TA to pTA*. Expert and Citizen Assessment of Science and Technology (ECAST). https://ecastnetwork.org/research/technology-assessment-and-public-participation-from-ta-to-pta/.

Worthington, R., Rask, M., & Minna, L. (eds.). (2012b). *Citizen Participation in Global Environmental Governance*. Routledge. https://doi.org/10.4324/9781315870458.

Wynne, B. (2006). Public engagement as a means of restoring public trust in science – Hitting the notes, but missing the music? *Community Genetics*, *9*(3), 211–220.

Yang, H., Dobbie, S., Ramirez-Villegas, J. et al. (2016). Potential negative consequences of geoengineering on crop production: A study of Indian groundnut. *Geophysical Research Letters*, *43*(22), 11,786–11,795. https://doi.org/10.1002/2016GL071209.

Acknowledgments

We are deeply grateful for the collective wisdom of many colleagues who have contributed to various portions of this Element. The genesis of this Element was a workshop held at Stanford University, in collaboration with the Stanford Deliberative Democracy Lab, in June 2023 in which most coauthors participated. This Element draws on insights generously offered (in person and/or remotely) at that workshop from Chad Baum, Louise Bedsworth, Benjamin Converse, Sally Klimp, Marcella Kolpin, Peter Irvine, Jane Long, Doug MacMartin, Juan Moreno-Cruz, Andy Parker, Ted Parson, Delaney Pues, Kate Ricke, Benjamin Sovacool, Masahiro Sugiyama, Pablo Saurez, Kristel Tjandra, and James Temple. We are also deeply grateful to several of those colleagues, as well as Ben Kravitz, for also reviewing and in the case of Marcella Kolpin, drafting, some of the briefing materials contained in this Element following that workshop. Finally, we thank our funders, the UC Santa Cruz Center for Coastal Climate Resilience, the UC Santa Cruz Center for Reimagining Leadership, the UC Santa Cruz Institute for Social Transformation, and the UC Santa Cruz Earth Futures Institute for their generous support of this project.

Cambridge Elements $\equiv$

Public Engagement with Science

Angela Potochnik
University of Cincinnati

Angela Potochnik is a Professor of philosophy and Director of the Center for Public Engagement with Science at the University of Cincinnati. Her research addresses the nature of science and its successes, the relationships between science and the public, and methods in population biology. She is the author of *Idealization and the Aims of Science* (Chicago, 2017), *Science and the Public* (Cambridge, 2024), and coauthor of *Recipes for Science* (Routledge, 2018), an introduction to scientific methods and reasoning.

Melissa Jacquart
University of Cincinnati

Melissa Jacquart is an Assistant Professor of philosophy and Curriculum & Pedagogy Director for the Center for Public Engagement with Science at the University of Cincinnati. Her research focuses on epistemological issues in the philosophy of science, philosophy of astrophysics, feminist philosophy, philosophy and education, and public engagement with science. She is a 2022–2023 Whiting Public Engagement Fellow.

About the Series

This interdisciplinary series draws from a broad range of research and professional expertise to guide theory and practice of public engagement with science, including science communication, formal and informal science education, community participation in scientific research, science policy, and other interfaces between science and the public.

Cambridge Elements ≡

Public Engagement with Science

Elements in the Series

A full series listing is available at: www.cambridge.org/PEWS

For EU product safety concerns, contact us at Calle de José Abascal, 56–1°, 28003 Madrid, Spain or eugpsr@cambridge.org.

www.ingramcontent.com/pod-product-compliance
Ingram Content Group UK Ltd.
Pitfield, Milton Keynes, MK11 3LW, UK
UKHW022147050526
470747UK00010BA/456